AN INTRODUCTION TO CHURCH HISTORY

AN INTRODUCTION
TO
CHURCH
HISTORY

by

Howard F. Vos

MOODY PRESS
CHICAGO

Revised and enlarged edition of the former title,
Highlights of Church History, which was first revised
in 1977 under the title *Beginnings in Church History*

All Scripture quotations are from the *New American Standard Bible,* © 1960,
1962, 1963, 1968, 1971, 1972, 1973, 1975, and 1977 by The Lockman Foundation.

Library of Congress Cataloging in Publication Data

Vos, Howard Frederic, 1925-
  An introduction to church history.

  Rev. ed. of: Beginnings in church history. Rev. ed. c1977.
  Bibliography: p. 203
  Includes index.
  1. Church history. I. Vos, Howard Frederic, 1925-
Beginnings in church history. II. Title. III. Title: Church history.
BR145.2.V68   1984   270   84-4516
ISBN 0-8024-0315-8

1 2 3 4 5 6 7 Printing EB Year 89 88 87 86 85 84

Printed in the United States of America

Contents

1

Beginnings

The Passover season was ended. The crowds that had gathered for the occasion dispersed, and Jerusalem returned to normal. Some were puzzled by the unusual circumstances surrounding the crucifixion of a certain Jesus of Nazareth, who appeared to be a revolutionist—for He had talked about setting up a kingdom of His own. A rumor had spread concerning His resurrection from the dead, but certainly that was impossible, they thought. Had not the soldiers who guarded His tomb reported the theft of His body by His followers? That was sufficient explanation for most. Another Galilean rabble rouser had come to a grisly end.

One hundred twenty of His followers who had gathered in an upper room knew otherwise. Having seen and talked with the risen Lord, they awaited at His command the coming of the Holy Spirit. On the day of Pentecost (fifty days after the crucifixion and ten days after the ascension), they were rewarded. A sound as of a rushing wind filled the house. On each of the group lighted what appeared to be a tongue of flame. Immediately they were filled with the Spirit and began to speak in other tongues. Rapidly word of this phenomenon spread among Jews gathered for the feast of Pentecost, and a crowd came rushing to investigate. Upon arrival each heard the message of truth in his own language. Some marveled. Others accused the disciples of being intoxicated. This was a foolish assertion, because drunkenness would only produce gibberish, not intelligible conversation in another language. Besides, it was early in the day—too early for such a large group to be drunk.

At this point Peter arose and addressed the throng. He pointed out that this remarkable phenomenon was a result of the Holy Spirit's ministry among them. Then he preached Christ: His death, resurrection, and ascension and the present necessity of receiving Him by faith as Savior and being baptized in His name. The Holy Spirit so wrought that three thousand believed on that memorable day.

Thus the church was born.[1] And wonderful was the experience of believers during succeeding days. They held to the true doctrine, were faithful in prayer, partook frequently of the Lord's Supper, enjoyed each other's fellowship, were in one accord, and lived joyous lives. Those who met them were strangely moved and awed; many believed *daily* (Acts 2:42-47). Soon the number of believers swelled to about five thousand men; there were probably women and children in addition (Acts 4:4).

But believers were not merely to enjoy a state of ecstasy. They were made aware of this by the persecution that the Temple priests initiated (Acts 4). Accepting the Lord was serious business; it involved suffering for His sake. Were they any better than He? The world hated Him; it would hate His followers also (John 15:18-19). Persecution came with increasing frequency and intensity. First there was warning, then beating, then murder. Stephen was the first Christian martyr (Acts 7:54-60). But persecution had the opposite of the desired effect. Members of the Jerusalem church were scattered all over Judea and Samaria, preaching as

1. It is recognized that not all agree the church originated at Pentecost. But note that one becomes a member of the church by means of the baptism of the Holy Spirit, which act joins him to the mystical Body of Christ (1 Corinthians 12:13 ff.). The baptism of the Holy Spirit was future in the gospels (Matthew 3:11; Mark 1:8; Luke 3:16; John 1:33; cf. Matthew 16:18) and in Acts 1:5, which states that the event would occur "not many days from now." It is past in Acts 11:15-16. Where else could one logically begin the baptism than at Pentecost? If the beginning of the baptism of the Holy Spirit, by which one becomes a member of the church, occurred at Pentecost, the church must have begun there.

they went. Philip went to Samaria to minister and witnessed a wonderful spiritual awakening there. The fulfillment of our Lord's commission to preach in Jerusalem, Judea, Samaria, and the uttermost part of the earth (Acts 1:8) was being realized.

At this point a certain Saul of Tarsus, a devout Pharisee who had been present at the stoning of Stephen, became a prominent persecutor of Christians. To stamp out the hated sect, he even determined to move against believers at Damascus. On the way north he was stopped dead in his tracks by the Lord he opposed (Acts 9). This vision of Christ and its accompanying conversion brought Saul an inner peace that he had failed to gain by conformity to Jewish law and a misdirected zeal in serving God. Traveling on to Damascus, Saul was filled with the Holy Spirit and received water baptism there. After that he spent three years in Arabia and subsequently returned to Damascus to preach his new-found faith. Under persecution he fled to Damascus and returned to Jerusalem. There he was stymied by the suspicion of believers until Barnabas persuaded the apostles that Saul's conversion was genuine. After a most useful time with Peter and James and a Jerusalem ministry that led to a plot on his life, Saul returned to Tarsus. For the next several years he preached in the region around his home and in Syria (Galatians 1:16-21; Acts 9:20-31). Meanwhile, the Palestinian church continued to grow, and Peter introduced the gospel to the Gentiles of Cornelius's household in Caesarea (Acts 10). The church in Syria expanded rapidly too, and believers were first called Christians at Antioch of Syria.

Ultimately, church growth at Antioch required more workers. Barnabas went to Tarsus to persuade Saul—later called Paul—to join in the ministry in the Syrian metropolis. Soon the Lord revealed to the church that He wanted the pair to engage in missionary activity. Barnabas and Paul departed, with the blessing of the whole church, to minister to Jews and Gentiles in the regions beyond. They traveled and preached in Cyprus and Asia Minor (modern Turkey) and returned to Antioch. When they arrived, a question of the relationship of Jew and Gentile in the church and to the law arose. Jewish Christians believed that Gentile believers had to submit to the law as well as place their faith in Christ. The issue was referred to the mother church at Jerusalem; Paul and Barnabas and others were sent there to present the case.

The decision of the great Council of Jerusalem (A.D. 49 or 50) is significant: "For it seemed good to the Holy Spirit, and to us to lay upon you no greater burden than these essentials: that you abstain from things sacrificed to idols and from blood and from things strangled and from fornication; if you keep yourselves free from such things, you will do well" (Acts 15:28-29). Under the guidance of the Holy Spirit, the council decided that the law, which had been an impossible burden for the Jew, should not be required of Gentiles.

On Paul's second missionary journey he was accompanied by Silas. The two again visited churches in Asia Minor and then, responding to the call of the man from Macedonia (Acts 16:9), they crossed over into Greece, where they established churches at Philippi, Thessalonica, Berea, and Corinth. Paul remained at Corinth for about eighteen months of successful evangelistic work. During this journey he also preached his famous sermon on Mars Hill (Acts 17).

On his third journey Paul again called on the believers in central Asia Minor. Traveling westward he stopped at Ephesus for about three years, where he carried the gospel banner to victory over the forces of Diana. After revisiting the churches in Greece, he returned to Jerusalem, where he was apprehended by the leaders of the Jews and imprisoned. At length, appealing to Caesar, he was taken to Rome for trial. There he was imprisoned for two years (apparently under a sort of house arrest, Acts 28:30), and there he enjoyed a fairly successful ministry to the many who had access to him. Tradition has it that Paul was released from prison and engaged in a fourth missionary journey, when he went to Spain and possibly southern France. He seems also to have gone to Crete, in addition to visiting some churches already established.

The other apostles were also active during the first century. Several apparently evangelized areas not already mentioned. Tradition teaches that Bartholomew preached in Armenia; Thomas in Parthia, Persia, and India; Matthew in Ethiopia; James the Younger in Egypt; Jude in Assyria and Persia; and Mark (not one of the apostles but closely related to them) in Alexandria. If the Babylon from which Peter wrote (1 Peter 5:13) was Babylon on the Euphrates instead of a symbolical representation of Rome, then Babylonia was also evangelized during the first century. Indications are that Peter ministered in Rome near the end of his life and was martyred there. Evidently, he also preached in several of the provinces of Asia Minor (1 Peter 1:1).

If there is any truth in these traditions concerning the apostles and other early church leaders, the gospel penetrated the more important inhabited areas of Europe, Asia, and Africa by the end of the first century.[2] In general support of this contention, Justin Martyr, one of the most outstanding leaders in the church about A.D. 150, observed:

> There is no people, Greek or barbarian, or of any other race, by whatever appellation or manners they may be distinguished, however ignorant of arts or agriculture, whether they dwell in tents or wander about in covered wagons, among whom prayers and thanksgivings are not offered in the name of the crucified Jesus to the Father and Creator of all things.[3]

Although admittedly this reference must have been primarily to lands within the Roman Empire, it does show a widespread dissemination of the gospel. In a real sense, then, the pattern of evangelism laid out in Acts 1:8 was realized: "But you shall receive power when the Holy Spirit has come upon you; and you shall be My witnesses both in Jerusalem, and in all Judea and Samaria, and even to the remotest part of the earth."

2. If India was evangelized during the first century, it is entirely reasonable to suppose that believers also reached China with the Christian message. Contacts between China and India were extensive at that time. Furthermore, Roman subjects traded directly with India and through middlemen with China during the first and second centuries after Christ. Since ideas flow along the arteries of trade, it is possible that the gospel reached the Far East in this way. There is also evidence that the Christian message appeared in Britain in the first century. On the general question of the spread of the gospel over the Roman Empire, remember that many lands were represented at Pentecost: Parthia, Media, Elam, Mesopotamia, Judea, Cappadocia, Pontus, Asia, Phrygia, Pamphylia, Egypt, Libya, Rome, Crete, and Arabia (Acts 2:9-11). Certainly these converts would witness of Christ upon return to their homelands. Also, Paul and others ministered in cities having a large percentage of transient people, e.g., Corinth, Ephesus, and Antioch.
3. William Hendriksen, *Colossians and Philemon* (Grand Rapids: Baker, 1964), 51.

2

The Fathers

As the apostles passed from the scene, others arose in the church to take their places. These leaders, generally elders or bishops, are called Fathers ("Fathers in God") because of the esteem in which they were held by church members or because of their historical relationship to later church developments. In fact, *Father* has come to apply to church leaders during an extended period, beginning about A.D. 95.

The Fathers frequently are divided into four groups: the Apostolic or Post-Apostolic Fathers (95-150); the Apologists (140-200); the Polemicists (180-225); and the Scientific Theologians (225-460). Sometimes they are classified as the Apostolic Fathers (second century); the Ante-Nicene Fathers (second and third centuries); the Nicene Fathers (fourth century); and the Post-Nicene Fathers (fifth century; sometimes to Gregory the Great in the West, 590; or John of Damascus in the East, c. 675). The Apostolic Fathers are characterized by edification, the Apologists by defense against attacks on Christianity, the Polemicists by attacks against heresy within the church, and the Scientific Theologians by a scientific study of theology in an effort to apply to theological investigation philosophical modes of thought then current.

The Apostolic Fathers

While the apostle John was writing Revelation on the Isle of Patmos or at Ephesus, Clement served as leading elder, or bishop, in the church at Rome. In this capacity he assumed responsibility for answering an appeal (as did Paul a half century earlier; cf. 1 Corinthians 7:1 ff.) from the church at Corinth for advice on how to restore harmony to a divided church. He sent a letter urging a demonstration of Christian graces in daily relationships and obedience to the elders and deacons against whom some were rebelling. He made frequent reference to both Old and New Testament Scripture and especially to Paul's epistles. Because this is the earliest extrabiblical Christian writing, it has attained a place of prominence among the writings of the Apostolic Fathers.

About a half century later another Roman, Hermas, wrote a work known as the *Shepherd of Hermas*. In it he records five visions that serve as the basis of a call to repentance from sins existent in the church of his day. In his description of these evils, Hermas gives a picture of the level of Christian living about A.D. 150. It is far from high. The book of *Second Clement* was probably written about the same time as the *Shepherd* and was not, therefore, the work of Clement of Rome. It is not really an epistle but a homily, probably delivered in Corinth, and is the oldest Christian sermon extant. Its message emphasizes practical Christian living and a sound view of Christ.

A Syrian Apostolic Father and the most famous of the group was Ignatius, bishop of Antioch. About 110, he was apprehended by Roman authorities because of his Christian profession and sent to Rome for martyrdom. Along the way he wrote letters to various churches. These seven letters were designed to promote unity in the churches addressed. Unity was to be accomplished on the one hand by rooting out heresies that denied the full divine-human personality of Christ, and on the other hand by the subjection of leaders in local congregations to a ruling bishop. Thus impetus was given to the power of bishops, but only over local congregations. He did not exalt the position of the bishop of Rome over that of other bishops, but he seems to have been the first to speak of a *Catholic* (universal) church.

In Asia Minor (modern Turkey) two Fathers were active: Polycarp and Papias. Polycarp, bishop of Smyrna (modern Izmir), is particularly interesting to modern Christians because he was a disciple of the apostle John. His letter to the Philippians remains. As one would expect from a disciple of John, Polycarp emphasized in his letter faith in Christ and the necessary outworking of that faith in daily living. Unlike those of his friend Ignatius, his concerns do not involve church organization and discipline. Papias, bishop of Hierapolis in Phrygia, wrote about 125. His *Interpretations of the Sayings (Oracles) of the Lord* is now lost, but parts of it survive in the writings of Irenaeus and Eusebius. These fragments deal with the life and teachings of Christ and attempt to preserve information obtained from those who had known Christ. They are especially interesting for their historical references, such as the statement that Mark got the information for his gospel from Peter.

Works assigned to the period of the Apostolic Fathers also originated in North Africa. *Barnabas* is generally considered to have been written in Alexandria—probably somewhere between A.D. 70 and 130. Like much of the other literature of Alexandria, this epistle is quite allegorical in nature, engaging in gross typology and numerology. The basic problem of the epistle concerns the necessity of a Christian's keeping the law. It holds that such was not necessary; the work of Christ was sufficient. It becomes so anti-Judaic as almost to deny a historical connection between Judaism and Christianity. The *Didache*, or *Teachings of the Twelve*, is also believed to have originated in Alexandria (though some think it came from Syria), probably during the first decades of the second century. A church manual, divided into three parts, the *Didache* treats Christian ethics, liturgical and disciplinary matters, and the need for a life of preparedness in view of the return of Christ.

The Apostolic Fathers must be evaluated in accordance with their apparent purpose: to exhort and edify the church. Sometimes they are criticized by evangelicals because they do not seem to grasp the New Testament concept of salvation by faith or because they seem to neglect certain doctrines. It should be remembered, however, that if one's purpose is to exhort to a higher plane of Christian living, he may make rather obscure allusions to the means by which one becomes a Christian. Moreover, informal utterances of pious faith are not designed to provide completeness of theological treatment and should not be judged by the same criteria as a systematic theology. Admittedly however, the Apostolic Fathers do in some instances assign a rather significant place to baptism as a medium of forgiveness of sin. Martyrdom and celibacy are also thought to have special sin-atoning power. On the whole the Apostolic Fathers picture a church still throbbing with missionary zeal, a church in which individual responsibility is still everywhere recognized, and a church in which hierarchal organization is at a minimum.

The Apostolic Fathers should be used with caution, however. Although they exhibit more than individual opinions and provide something of a cross section of doctrinal beliefs and conduct in the churches, the sampling is minimal. All their writings for this half century of time fill only one moderate-sized volume. And since the layman was not vocal, we know only what the clergy thought about what was going on in a few churches. What they thought may not have approximated true conditions. And of course there is no way of knowing whether these churches or churchmen were typical or extreme examples of the period.

The Apologists

The approach and purpose of the Apologists were entirely different from those of the Apostolic Fathers. The Apologists sought to win legal recognition for Christianity and to defend it against certain charges leveled by the pagan populace. In constructing this defense[1] the Apologists wrote in a more philosophical vein than the Apostolic Fathers. A generation of Christians from a higher social class and with more extensive education had arisen. As the Apologists wrote their defenses they had at hand two literary forms already in use in the Roman world: the legal

---

1. *Apology* in its basic meaning signifies "defense"; it is so used by the Apologists. The fact that the word has taken on the connotation of "making excuse" should not confuse the reader.

speech *(apologia)* delivered before judicial authorities and subsequently published, and the literary dialogue.

In seeking to win a favorable position for Christianity, the Apologists tried on the one hand to demonstrate the superiority of the Hebrew-Christian tradition over paganism, and on the other to defend Christianity against certain charges. They viewed this superiority as both temporal and spiritual. Justin Martyr claimed that Moses wrote the Pentateuch long before the Trojan War (c. 1250 B.C.), thus antedating Greek history, to say nothing of Roman. And he and other Apologists made much of fulfillment of prophecy in an attempt to show that Christianity was not something new, but merely a continuation or culmination of the ancient Hebrew faith. As to the spiritual superiority of Christianity over paganism, the Apologists claimed that noble pagans had obtained their high ideals from God or Moses.

Charges against which Apologists defended Christianity were atheism, cannibalism, immorality, and antisocial action. The first charge arose because Christians refused to worship the emperor or the Greco-Roman gods; the second, because of a misunderstanding of the celebration of the Lord's Supper; the third, because religious services generally had to be conducted in secret or after dark and because Christians displayed great love for each other; and the last, because Christians found it necessary to retire from much of public life, as most aspects of human existence were in some way connected with worship of the gods. For instance, one who held public office had to participate in and even lead the populace in sacrifices to the ruler or the goddess Roma. Normally when one attended an athletic festival or a drama, he found himself acquiescing in a sacrifice to a god before the event began.

In their effort to win recognition from the state for their faith, the Apologists generally took a philosophical approach. It was only natural that they should do so, because on the one hand they were trying to reason out the case for Christianity with their opponents, and because on the other hand they often wrote to men who were themselves greatly interested in philosophy. (Note, for instance, that the emperor Marcus Aurelius was a Stoic philosopher, and apologies were addressed to him.) Because of their philosophical orientation, the Apologists have been accused of undue surrender to the world view of heathenism. Even their teachings about Jesus Christ appear in the form of the Logos doctrine. To the philosophers the Logos was an impersonal controlling and developing principle of the universe. But John in chapter one of his gospel had also used *Logos* to describe Christ, without any sacrifice of His deity or the value of His atoning work. And the Apologists on most points seem to have upheld the New Testament concept of Jesus Christ, though it must be admitted that such writers as Justin sometimes described Christ as a being of inferior rank to the Father. The very fact that the Apologists placed such great stress on the Logos demonstrates that their theology was Christ centered. Moreover, although the practice may involve dangers, it is neither wrong nor undesirable to make one's message intelligible to one's age.

Probably the most dramatic and therefore the best known of the Apologists was Justin Martyr. Certainly he was a great literary defender of the faith. Born about A.D. 100 in a small town in Samaria, Justin early became well acquainted with the various philosophical systems. But his great knowledge of these philosophies also led him to a realization of their inadequacies. At this point of disillusionment and searching, an old Christian came into Justin Martyr's life and showed him the way of faith in Christ. Thereafter, the converted philosopher became a Christian philosopher, presenting the Christian message in philosophical terms. He wrote apologies to the emperor Antoninus Pius and his adopted son, Marcus Aurelius, and a dialogue with Trypho the Jew. In the apologies, he sought to defend Christianity against the charges of atheism and immorality, to demonstrate that Christians were loyal citizens (Christ's kingdom was not of this world; so the empire had no reason to fear insurrection), and to prove that the truth was taught by Christianity alone. In his dialogue with Trypho, Justin tried to show that Jesus was the Messiah. During his second stay in Rome, Justin engaged in a public debate with a philosopher by the name of Crescens. Shortly thereafter (c. 163), Justin was martyred by Marcus Aurelius, perhaps at the instigation of several philosophers close to the emperor.

One of Justin's converts in Rome was Tatian, a writer skilled in argumentation. His *Address to the Greeks* was largely a tirade against paganism; it ridiculed almost every pagan practice. In the latter part, he argued that since Christianity was superior to Greek religion and thought, it deserved to be tolerated. After Justin's martyrdom, Tatian drifted off into the error of Gnosticism (for a discussion see chap. 3). Tatian is probably best known for his *Diatessaron,* the earliest harmony of the gospels, composed about A.D. 150-60.

Another writer of note sometimes classified among the Apologists was Tertullian. Born in Carthage about 160, he later moved to Rome, where he became a lawyer, and was subsequently won to Christianity. His *Apologeticus,* addressed to the Roman governor of Carthage, refuted the common charges leveled against Christians, demonstrated the loyalty of Christians to the empire, and showed that persecution of Christians was foolish anyway, because they multiplied whenever persecuted. About 200, Tertullian became enmeshed in the error of Montanism (for a discussion see chap. 3). These three were the more important of the Apologists, but fragmentary or fairly complete writings of at least a half dozen others do exist.

The Polemicists

As the Christian movement grew older, errors arose within its ranks—errors that called forth defenders of the faith and that by reaction led to the development of Christian doctrine and the formulation of a New Testament canon. It is significant that in refuting error the Polemicists appealed extensively to New Testament books as the source of true doctrine. Thus they gave impetus to the later official pronouncements on the contents of the New Testament canon. The work of the Polemicists also gave rise to the concept of an orthodox catholic church opposed to heresy. Since a large part of the next chapter is devoted to a definition of those errors, note is made here only of some chief attackers of them.

Although most of the Apologists lived in the East, most of the Polemicists lived in the West. Earliest of these was Irenaeus, who wrote *Against Heresies* about 185, at Lyons, France. Primarily aimed against the philosophical error of Gnosticism, this work may be characterized as follows: Book I—a historical sketch of Gnostic sects presented in conjunction with a statement of Christian faith; Book II—a philosophical critique of Gnosticism; Book III—a scriptural critique of Gnosticism; Book IV—answers to Gnosticism from the words of Christ; Book V—a vindication of the resurrection against Gnostic arguments.

Covering much the same ground as Irenaeus, Hippolytus also attacked Gnosticism, as well as other errors, in his *Refutation of All Heresies* (written about 200). Although Hippolytus may have borrowed from Irenaeus, he significantly supplements the work of the latter. Hippolytus came into conflict with the dominant party in Rome because he criticized them for disciplinary laxity and doctrinal unsoundness. In particular, he linked Callixtus, an important pastor, with Noetianism and Sabellianism—defective forms of Trinitarian teaching.

In Carthage lived two other Western Polemicists: Tertullian and Cyprian. Tertullian may be classified with the Apologists if one emphasizes his *Apologeticus* or as a Scientific Theologian if one emphasizes his *De Anima* (concerning the origin of the soul). In fact, he is commonly regarded as the founder of Latin (Roman Catholic) theology. But he is classified here because of his intensely passionate opposition to paganism, Judaism, early forms of Unitarianism, and Gnosticism. It has been said that he did more than anyone else to overthrow Gnosticism. Although Tertullian lapsed into the Montanistic error, he renewed fellowship with the church before his death. Tertullian's ministry was carried on during the first decades of the third century.

Cyprian (martyred in 258) in his polemic activity is known for his opposition to Novatianism. Novatus (Novatian) held that those who lapsed during persecution could not be pronounced forgiven by the church and restored to its fellowship; forgiveness must be left to God alone. It was not Novatus's severity of discipline but his denial that the church had the right to grant absolution that caused his excommunication. The church had become conscious of her catholicity and unity by this time, and those who would not submit to divinely appointed bishops were regarded as heretics. In line with this common attitude, Cyprian, bishop of Cathage, felt duty bound to condemn Novatus.

Sometimes leaders of the school of Alexandria are listed among the Polemicists. Clement's *Protepticus* is an apologetic missionary document written to demonstrate the superiority of Christianity to paganism. Origen wrote his *Against Celsus* to answer certain charges against Christianity. But it is the opinion of the writer that these men are more properly classified among the Scientific Theologians.

The Scientific Theologians

As has been noted already, the Scientific Theologians sought to apply current modes of thought to theological investigation. Moreover, they tried to develop scientific methods of biblical interpretation and textual criticism. The classification of these writers falls roughly into three groups. (1) Those living in Alexandria (Pantaenus, Clement, Origen, and, later, Athanasius, Cyril, et al.) were the most speculative in approach; (2) writers of the West (Jerome, Ambrose, Augustine) tended to emphasize the authority of the church and its tradition; and (3) those ministering in Asia Minor and Syria (Theodore of Mopsuestia, John Chrysostom, et al.) took a generally literal approach to biblical study.

ALEXANDRIAN THEOLOGIANS

Earliest of the leaders of the school in Alexandria for converts from paganism and children of believers was Pantaenus, who held the reins of authority until 200. Since the writings of Pantaenus no longer exist (or have not yet been discovered), it is necessary to move to a discussion of his more famous successors. Associated with Pantaenus from 190, Clement headed the school of Alexandria from 200 to 202, when he was forced by persecution to leave the city. His writings include *Address to the Greeks, The Tutor, The Miscellanies,* and the *Outlines of Scripture Interpretation.* The first was designed to win converts from heathenism; the second, to provide new converts with simple instruction for living the Christian life; the third, to show the superiority of

Christianity to pagan philosophy; and the last, to provide commentaries on various scriptural passages, partly in answer to heretical interpretations. In the writings of Clement, the influence of Greek philosophy is prominent, especially that of Plato; but the Bible also has a place of importance. He sought to synthesize Christianity and Greek philosophy and is significant in church history as being the first to present Christianity in the forms of secular literature for the Christian community.

Most famous of the Alexandrian writers was Origen, who led the school from 202 to 232. Thereafter he moved to Caesarea in Palestine, where he continued his illustrious career for another twenty years until the Decian persecution. Origen brought to scientific formulation the allegorical interpretation of Scripture. The germs of this approach may be seen in Philo of Alexandria, a contemporary of Christ who had sought to find a reconciliation between Greek philosophy and Jewish thought by searching for hidden meanings in the Old Testament. Christian writers after Philo employed the allegorical method, but Origen receives the credit for the full development of the approach. Simply described, it holds that the literal meaning of Scripture conceals a deeper meaning, available only to the mature believer. The hidden meaning that he found sometimes bore little or no relationship to the literal. This concealing of truth by God under the guise of commonly understood words was designed to prevent pearls from being cast before swine.

Origen's works number in the thousands (some say six thousand, including letters and articles), involving critical, apologetic, dogmatic, and practical treatises. His commentaries deal with almost the whole Bible. Although they are helpful at points, their value is restricted by his allegorisms. Highly significant are his critical or textual studies: the *Hexapla* and *Tetrapla*. The former has several Hebrew and Greek versions arranged in parallel columns. The latter contains the four Greek versions of the *Hexapla*. Only fragments of these works remain. Origen's *On First Principles* is the earliest systematic theology that has come down to us.

While Origen made some positive contributions to the theology of the church, he is more commonly known for views that did not receive general acceptance. For instance, he taught that the souls of men existed as fallen spirits before the birth of the individuals, which teaching accounted for man's sinful nature. Second, he held that in His atonement Christ paid a ransom to Satan, by whom all were enslaved in the bondage of sin. Third, he believed that the rejected, who go to hell at death, would experience there a purifying fire that ultimately would cleanse even the wicked; all would ultimately reach the state of bliss, including the devil himself.

Many decades later the great Athanasius (c. 293-373) rose to a position of leadership in Alexandria. To him goes special credit for the triumph of the orthodox view of Christ over Arianism, "a thinly disguised paganism," at the Council of Nicea in 325 (see chap. 4). Even prior to the outbreak of the Arian controversy, he had become a recognized theologian for his production of *Contra Gentiles* and *On the Incarnation*. In 326 he became bishop of Alexandria and thereafter steadfastly defended the Nicene position on the full deity of Christ.

A later figure of significance in Alexandria was Cyril (376-444). Becoming patriarch of Alexandria in 412, he devoted himself to the defense of the orthodox doctrine of the person of Christ, but often did so in a highhanded and unprincipled manner. He was a zealous advocate of veneration of the virgin Mary.

WESTERN THEOLOGIANS

One of the greatest of the Western Fathers was Jerome (c. 345-420). Born in northeastern Italy, he spent several years in Rome, studying languages and philosophy, and was baptized at the age of nineteen. During the next twenty years he moved around a great deal—in Gaul, the East, and Italy—perfecting his knowledge of Greek and Hebrew and becoming a convert to monasticism. Settling in Bethlehem in 386, he began his influential writing ministry. By means of extensive correspondence and dramatic telling of the lives of early ascetics, he did much to promote asceticism and celibacy. As a writer against heresies Jerome was primarily the interpreter of accepted church dogma; he was not original. He wrote commentaries on almost all the books of the Bible, but they were unequal in value. He utilized allegorism, according to his admission, when he was unable to discover the literal meaning. Jerome ranks first among early exegetes, and his knowledge of languages was unsurpassed in the early church. He was careful about his sources of information. He knew and used extensively early versions and manuscripts of the Bible no longer extant. Operating on the principle that only the original text of Scripture is free from error, he engaged in considerable manuscript study in order to determine what, among variant readings, should be considered the original and true text. Out of these efforts came the work for which he is best known: the Vulgate, a translation of the Bible into Latin. Jerome also tried to bring Eusebius's *Ecclesiastical History*[2] up to date by recording events for the years 325-378.

Ambrose, bishop of Milan (374-97), was another of the most illustrious Fathers of the Western church. Because his writings represent an official witness to the teachings of the Roman church in his own time and earlier centuries, they have been constantly appealed to by popes, councils, and theologians. Commentaries on Scripture constitute more than half of his writings. In these commentaries Ambrose employs the allegorico-mystical method of interpretation: he admits a literal sense, but seeks everywhere a deeper mystical meaning that he converts into practical instruction for Christian life. Ambrose is also known for his contributions in music. But apparently tradition has been too kind to him. So far no documents have been brought to light to prove he composed anything but the tunes to most of his hymns. And although a large number of hymns have been attributed to him, fewer than twenty can be assigned to him with certainty. In a day when church services were becoming increasingly liturgical and choirs were assuming greater importance, Ambrose championed congregational singing. He also en-

2. Eusebius of Caesarea lived about 260-341 and composed a church history that serves as a mine of information about the early church. Although it is not a great literary work or a well-balanced work (the writer's meager knowledge of Latin prevented him from knowing much about the Western church), the *Ecclesiastical History* does provide a great deal of information that otherwise would be lost to us. His testimony concerning the canon is particularly valuable.

couraged monasticism. In his diligence in teaching the faith and refuting heresy, he influenced many, not the least of whom was St. Augustine.

St. Augustine, bishop of Hippo in North Africa, stands preeminent among theologians of all time. His influence upon all faiths has been significant. His emphasis on a personal experience of the grace of God as necessary to salvation has caused Protestants to accept him as a forerunner of the Reformation. His emphasis on the church, her creed, and sacraments has appealed to Romanists. His teaching that the Millennium was the period between Christ's first and second comings, during which time the church would conquer the world, has contributed greatly to amillennial and postmillennial theologies of past and present. Augustine's teaching that man is in all his parts perverted by sin profoundly influenced Calvinistic theology. And such an outstanding American scholar as Perry Miller made the claim in his *New England Mind* that the Puritans were even more Augustinian than Calvinistic in their theology. Augustine's views on the nature of man and his salvation are described further in chapter 4.

Augustine (354-430) came from a respectable but not a rich family. His life, a journey through periods of immorality, entanglement in appealing philosophies and heresies of the day, and spiritual crisis to the achievement of moral and spiritual victory, is one of the best-known biographies of all time. The account, recorded in his *Confessions,* has been read by millions. *Confessions* is Augustine's moral autobiography; *Revisions* is his intellectual autobiography, which describes the changes in his thought over the years. Most important of his theological works is his *Concerning the Trinity; Concerning Christian Doctrine* is the most important of his exegetical works. His philosophy of history, the first to be developed, is found in his *City of God.* In it he traces the development of the city of earth and the city of God through biblical and secular history and shows the destiny of the two cities: the former to eternal punishment and the latter to eternal bliss. He portrays the sovereignty of God in the affairs of men and the ultimate triumph of good over evil, though currently the reverse is often true.

THEOLOGIANS OF ASIA MINOR AND SYRIA

Three of the most important leaders of the church in Asia Minor and Syria were the Three Great Cappadocians of central Asia Minor. These men are known for their contribution to the development of the doctrine of the Trinity and the defense of the orthodox position in church. Of these three, Basil the Great (330-97) of Caesarea is known for his opposition to heresies, especially Arianism, and for the organization of Eastern monasticism. His brother, Gregory of Nyssa (332-398), was a champion of orthodoxy at the Council of Constantinople in 381 and is respected as one of the founders of the Eastern Church. Gregory of Nazianzus (329-90) became bishop of Constantinople in 380 and for some years headed the orthodox cause.

Two other important Scientific Theologians in the Eastern Church were John Chrysostom and Theodore. Theodore (350-428) was bishop of Mopsuestia in Cilicia (Asia Minor) for thirty-six years. A brilliant exegete, he wrote commentaries on most books of the Bible, generally following grammatico-historical and realistic explanations of the text. This method of interpreting the words of Scripture according to their ordinary grammatical meaning and in the light of their historical background was the prevailing mode of interpretation in the Antiochene school of thought, from which background Theodore had come. John Calvin was later to become famous for his contributions to the grammatico-historical method of biblical interpretation. Theodore reputedly was the first to attempt to place the Psalms in their historical context.

John Chrysostom (347-407), the most prominent doctor of the Greek church, also was important as a representative of the grammatico-historical interpretation of Scripture in opposition to the allegorical and mystical interpretations of Alexandria. While Chrysostom did not exclude all allegorical and mystical elements from scriptural study, he confined them to cases in which he felt the inspired author suggested such a meaning. Chrysostom is also important for the reformation of Eastern theology. At the time of the Reformation there were long discussions whether Chrysostom was Protestant or Catholic. Though he ignored confession to a priest, he did hold to the real presence in the Eucharist, to the one church, and to tradition as a valid basis of authority. Born in Antioch and for some years preacher in the cathedral there, Chrysostom became patriarch of Constantinople near the end of his life. Perhaps he is best known for his preaching. The name *Chrysostom* (golden-mouthed) was bestowed upon him for his eloquence. Copies of some six hundred fifty of his sermons still exist.

A study of the Fathers is very valuable for one interested in the development of church doctrine and organization. In their lives and teachings we find the seed plot of almost all that arose later. In germ form appear the dogmas of purgatory, transubstantiation, priestly mediation, baptismal regeneration, and the whole sacramental system. They defined the allegorical, mystical, and literal interpretations of Scripture. To them we look for a formulation of the hierarchal system and the importance of the church as the sphere of salvation. But through them also came the development of the canon and formulation of the great creeds of Christendom, which serve as the basis of most successive teaching concerning the Trinity, the person of Christ, and the nature of the Holy Spirit. And among them arose great defenders of the faith; they answered the persecutors of Christianity and attacked heretics who attempted to destroy the faith from within. It is to the persecutions and perversions of the faith that we now turn.

3

Foes Without and Within

The Persecutions

The Christian movement was hardly launched when it faced its first persecutors. This was to be expected, for Jesus Himself had warned His disciples, "If they persecuted Me, they will also persecute you" (John 15:20). Shortly after Pentecost the success of apostolic preaching so jolted members of the Sanhedrin that they threw Peter and John into prison (Acts 4). Soon thereafter they imprisoned the whole apostolic band (Acts 5). Opposition heightened, resulting in the stoning of Stephen (Acts 7). A few years later, probably A.D. 44, Herod Agrippa I slew James the brother of John (Acts 12:2) and imprisoned Peter. So it was with the Jews that persecution of the church began.

Reasons for their opposition to the gospel are not hard to discover. Jewish leaders feared a rapidly rising movement that would decimate their constituency. And evidently many among them, like Saul of Tarsus, honestly believed that Christianity was a perversion of true Judaism and that they were honoring God by attacking it. Moreover, some Jews might have worried about losing their privileged position in the empire if Palestine were infected with individuals who spoke about another kingdom ruled by a king other than Caesar. And a few, of the Zealot variety, may have opposed Christianity because it was not willing to join

Jewish nationalistic moves for independence.

Reasons for Roman persecution were much more complex. Christians were politically suspect because they spoke of a kingdom with Christ as its ruler. Materialistically minded Romans took statements concerning such a kingdom to imply a plan for overthrow of the government. Moreover, there was a union of religion and state in ancient Rome; so refusal to worship the goddess Roma or the divine emperor constituted treason. And no government has ever dealt lightly with treason.

Christians suffered social ostracism because they came, especially in the early days, largely from the lowest classes of society and because as good Christians they could not participate in much of the public life of their time. For example, as civil servants they might be required to join in ceremonies in honor of the divine Caesar. Even engaging in sporting and theatrical events was impossible, because sacrifice to a pagan deity normally occurred before a drama or an athletic festival. They also condemned public games in which gladiators fought in mortal combat to entertain spectators and in which innocent prisoners were thrown to wild beasts for entertainment of the crowds. And the fact that Christians proclaimed the equality of all men before God put them in direct opposition to the generally accepted institution of slavery.

There were also economic reasons for the persecution of Christians. Priests, idol makers, and other vested religious interests could hardly look on disinterestedly while their incomes dwindled and their very livelihoods stood in jeopardy. Since leaders of the old religions held important positions in society, they could easily stir up mob opposition to Christianity. The success of Demetrius and the other idol makers of Ephesus in this regard is a case in point (Acts 19). Christians were also made scapegoats for great calamities such as famine, earthquakes, and pestilence—which were sometimes regarded as punishment meted out because people had forsaken the Greco-Roman gods.

Religiously, Christianity suffered because it was exclusive, not tolerant like other faiths of the empire. In fact it was aggressive in trying to win adherents from other faiths. And because Christians had to hold religious observances in secret, it was easy for all sorts of rumors to circulate about them. Some saw in their love for each other an evidence of licentiousness. Other interpreted their statements used in connection with Communion to refer to cannibalism.

The event that sparked official persecutions, however, was the fire of Rome, July of A.D. 64. That holocaust, which lasted for nine days and gutted ten of the fourteen districts of the city, brought untold suffering to a population of some one million. Some of Nero's enemies circulated a report that he had started the fire. The charge was probably untrue, but Nero diverted attention from himself by making scapegoats out of the Christian community in Rome. The penalty suffered by many of the supposed incendiaries was burning at the stake at night to light the gardens near Nero's circus in the Vaticanus section of Rome. Some were thrown to wild beasts or mad dogs. Paul suffered martyrdom at the hands of Nero; Peter is said to have suffered the same fate. The Neronian persecution is important because it established the precedent and the manner of persecuting Christians, though it did not lead to any persecution outside Rome.

The second persecution broke out in A.D. 95, during the reign of Domitian. It was originally directed against Jews who refused to pay a tax designed to help fund construction of the magnificent new temple to Jupiter on the Capitoline Hill in Rome. Being associated with Judaism still, Christians also suffered during this persecution. Moreover, Domitian enforced emperor worship. Upon refusal to participate Christians were charged with treason. Some were martyred, some dispossessed of property, and others banished. It was at this time that the apostle John was exiled to the Isle of Patmos, where he received the vision of the Revelation. It is not clear that John's exile was instigated by the emperor, however; probably local opposition in the province of Asia was responsible for that.

Definite imperial policy concerning persecution was not developed until early in the second century. Pliny the Younger, a Roman lawyer, served as governor of the provinces of Bithynia and Pontus in Asia Minor, 111-113. While there, Pliny faced a great defection from paganism and a corresponding growth of the Christian movement. He felt obligated to deal with this situation and concluded that those brought before him for trial should be asked three times if they were Christians, each time the question being accompanied with threats. If they persisted in their faith after the third repetition of the question, they were to be led out and executed. Uncertain of the rightness of his procedure, Pliny wrote to the emperor Trajan for advice. Trajan replied that Christians were not to be sought out; but if reported and convicted they were to be punished, unless they repented and worshiped the gods. Anonymous information was not to be received against them. Thus an official policy was established. Soon governors throughout the empire were following the principles Trajan had enunciated. Many believers were martyred, including the famous Ignatius, bishop of Antioch, who was thrown to wild beasts in Rome about 115.

During the reign of Trajan's successor, Hadrian (117-138), the general policy of Trajan was followed; Christians were persecuted in moderation. When it became common for mobs at heathen festivals to demand the blood of Christians, Hadrian published an edict against such riots. Christianity made marked progress in numbers, wealth, learning, and social influence during his reign.

Antoninus Pius (139-161) seems rather to have favored Christians; but he felt he had to uphold the established imperial policy concerning them. So there were many martyrs, including Polycarp, bishop of Smyrna. It should be noted that in many instances during his reign, and particularly in the case of Polycarp, local mobs were responsible for much of the persecution. A good observation that applies to the reign of Antoninus as well as to that of the other Roman emperors, is that the persecutions of Christians were always of limited extent and that their ferocity was dependent on local conditions and the attitude of the provincial governors.

A new approach to persecution arose during the reign of Marcus Aurelius (161-180). An intolerant Stoic, he had no sympathy with the concept of immorality. The exultation of Christian martyrs he attributed to their desire for theatrical display. Instead of waiting for accusation to be brought against Christians, as Trajan had done, Marcus Aurelius introduced a spy system designed to accumulate evidence against them. He put no check on the riots instituted against Christians. During his reign the practice of blaming the occurrence of earthquakes, famines, floods, and pestilences on Christians began. Supposedly these calamities befell the populace because they forsook the old gods and tolerated Christianity. Persecution under Marcus Aurelius was cruel and barbarous. Thousands were beheaded or thrown to wild beasts, including the famous Justin Martyr.

But even the Aurelian persecution was not an organized, empire-wide persecution for the extermination of Christianity. Neither could the efforts of Septimius Severus (193-211) and Maximinus (235-238) be considered an all-out war on Christianity. Septimius Severus directed his attack primarily against Egypt and North Africa, and even there he was largely interested in putting a stop to proselytizing. Maximinus sought to wipe out Christian leaders only in certain areas.

In the middle of the third century the situation changed, however. Rome celebrated the thousandth anniversary of her founding and looked back to the days of prosperity, stability, and unquestioned authority in the Mediterranean world. How the gods had once favored her! Now the foundations of the economic, political, and social structure were crumbling. Public calamities such as earthquakes and pestilences abounded. Barbarians hovered on the frontiers. A superstitious populace was easily persuaded that the gods were angry because so many Christians had left the old faith.

The emperor Decius (249-251) was convinced that the maintenance of a state religion was necessary for political stability and return of prosperity. Therefore in the first year of his reign he gave orders that all inhabitants of the empire should come before special officers and declare their allegiance to the gods, proving it with an act of sacrifice. This amounted to a petition on the part of the entire populace for blessing on the emperor and the seriously threatened empire. Of course this edict flushed out true Christians, who refused to sacrifice. They became enemies of the emperor, the state, and the public good and were subjected to severe persecution. Evidence shows that the design was not to destroy Christians but to reconvert them to the state cult. First to be seized were the higher clergy, in order to render the church leaderless and reduce its effectiveness. Multitudes recanted, because a conventional Christianity had already come into existence and the church was filled with individuals possessing only a superficial belief. But hosts of others suffered martyrdom. After about a year it became evident that the Decian persecution could not succeed. It was over by April 1, 251. In July the emperor died in battle and his edicts no longer had any force.

Decius's successor, Valerian (253-260), was at first friendly to Christianity; but after a number of public calamities, he was encouraged to resort to severe punishment of Christians to stop the trouble. Many great leaders lost their lives.

From 260 to 303 Christianity enjoyed respite from persecution. Then all fury broke loose. The emperor Diocletian, persuaded by Galerius, his colleague in the East, issued a series of edicts in 303 that commanded destruction of Christian places of worship and sacred books and imprisonment of the clergy. During the following year Christians were offered the alternative of renouncing their faith and offering pagan sacrifices or suffering martyrdom. In the eastern part of the empire persecution was especially brutal. Diocletian's co-ruler in the West, Maximian, carried out the edicts with full force in Italy and Africa. But Maximian's subordinate, Constantius, who ruled Gaul, Britain, and Spain, refused to execute anyone for his religion. The persecution ended for the most part in 305, when Diocletian abdicated the throne and retired to private life.

During the confused time that followed, Constantius's son, Constantine, rose to leadership in the western part of the empire. In 313 he and Licinius, as joint rulers of the empire, issued an edict giving full toleration to the Christian faith. Though Licinius subsequently reneged on his commitment and stirred up persecution in the East, full toleration of Christianity came to the entire empire when Constantine became sole ruler of the Roman world in 324. Constantine made Christianity a legal religion and favored its development in many ways, but it was not until near the end of the fourth century that Theodosius made Christianity the official religion of the empire and persecution of paganism began. In 392 he forbade heathen worship under severe penalties.

An accommodation occurred between Christianity and paganism during the latter decades of the fourth century. Though Christianity was winning a victory of sorts over paganism, paganism achieved victories of her own by infiltrating the Christian church in numerous subtle ways. As opposition to paganism increased, many took their place in the church without experiencing conversion. Thus large segments of church membership consisted merely of baptized pagans. The distinction between Christianity and paganism became increasingly blurred as the state church was established under the ultimate authority of the emperor. Under the circumstances it seems unwise to speak of the church's conquering the Roman Empire. One might as easily argue that the empire had conquered the church.

Accounts of the deaths of martyrs during the period of the Roman persecutions have been greatly dramatized. Their faith and courage were magnificent, but theirs was the easy way. Much greater suffering was endured by those who lay in their own filth in heavy irons in hot Eastern prisons, with little water or food, until they died of disease or starvation. Equally hard was the lot of those sentenced to work the fields and mines. Half naked, underfed, beaten for low production, the damp ground their bed, these believers faced a living death.

The persecutions had their effects. Usually the good effects are noted. Many were won to Christ through the manner of the death of the martyrs. Tertullian is often quoted: "The blood of the martyrs is the seed of the Church." It is also frequently noted that the church was more apt to be pure if one was in danger of his life for naming the name of Jesus; one would not lightly join for social or economic reasons. Moreover, persecution often forced Christians to flee to areas where normally they would not have gone; thus the gospel spread more widely. Persecution also helped to settle the question of what belonged in the New Testament canon. It is obvious that no one would give his life for something that was not Scripture; and under the difficult conditions of persecution, one was less likely to take the trouble to copy or preserve works of insignificant value. Last, under the duress of persecution church leaders called Apologists produced reasoned defenses of Christianity that countless generations since have used in defending their own faith.

But the persecutions had their ill effects too. Christians were so busy protecting themselves that there was little opportunity to leave a literary legacy. And a great problem arose in the church over the question of the lapsed. All did not hold true to the faith. Some buckled under persecution and then later reaffirmed their faith and wished to be reinstated to the fellowship of believers. Some believers favored restoration and some did not. Many churches split over the question. Also, the very experience of martyrdom became warped as to its purpose or benefits. Many came to believe that dying for the faith had some sin-atoning merit.

Early Heresies

It is probably true that one's greatest enemies are always internal. External opposition or difficulty will not ultimately overpower if internal strength is adequate for the test. So it was with the early church. The persecutions for the most part only brought about the increase of Christians, but the internal errors of the second and third centuries took a great toll of the faithful.

One of the earliest errors was Ebionism. Appearing in fully developed form in the second century, it was in reality only a continuation and amplification of the Judaistic opposition of the apostle Paul. In his letter to the Galatians he sternly rebuked those who sought salvation through law keeping. But human nature being what it is, men have always been enamored with religious systems that promise salvation by means of good works; and Ebionism was such a system. Ebionism grew up in Palestine and assumed various forms. Some groups seem to have been quite clear on the essentials of salvation but insistent on law keeping as a way of life. Most, however, appear to have denied the deity of Christ, His virgin birth, and the efficacy of His sufferings. These views they held in an effort to retain a true monotheism. To them Christ was unusual in His strict law observance, and He was rewarded with messiahship for His legal piety. The Ebionites generally rejected Paul's apostleship and his writings and tended to venerate Peter as the apostle to the circumcision. They put much stress on the law in general and on circumcision and Sabbath keeping in particular. One branch taught a kind of Jewish-Christian Gnosticism. Ebionism practically disappeared by the fifth century. It had little if any lasting effect on the church.

Like Ebionism, Gnosticism seems to have existed in germ form in the days of Paul and John. For instance, Colossians 2:8, 18-19 and much of 1 John well may have been aimed at this error. Gnosticism was a product of the spirit of religious fusion that characterized the first century. It borrowed elements from Judaism, Christianity, Greek philosophy, and Oriental mysticism and constructed a system of thought that sought to combine revelation with the "wisdom of this world." Spawned primarily in Egypt and Syria, it spread to Rome, Asia Minor, Mesopotamia, and Persia.

Gnostics taught that matter was evil and spirit was good. Therefore they were faced with the problem of how a good God could create an evil world. A system of emanations was their answer. That is, there emanated from God an infinite chain of beings that became increasingly evil. Finally, at the end of the line came the Demiurge, or somewhat evil God, who was identified with the Jehovah of the Old Testament, and who was thought to be the Creator of the world and man. The good God took pity on man in his plight and sent the highest emanation, Christ, to minister to man's need of salvation. Especially, Christ came as an emissary of light from the kingdom of light to dispel man's spiritual darkness. Atonement through His death was not considered necessary. Because matter was evil, the Messiah's body was considered by some to be only an appearance, by others to be merely a human body that the Messiah used from His baptism until His death on the cross.

Gnosticism derived its name from a Greek word for knowledge, and emphasis in the system was laid on attaining knowledge of the good God—which would insure salvation. The system was extremely aristocratic. It taught that the true Gnostics, of whom there were few, were born with a high degree of intuitive knowledge of God. Christ's teachings would help them to overcome the material world and enable them to establish communication with God and gain entrance into the kingdom of light. Ordinary church members could attain salvation by faith and good works. But the mass of humanity did not have a chance to be saved. Of great value to the true Gnostic and the average church member in attaining an experience of God was initiation into the mysteries of marriage to Christ, baptism, and other mystical rites of the church. The path of redemption also involved a low estimate of the flesh. Some punished the body by extreme asceticism; others gave full rein to the carnal desires of the flesh, for they felt that in such a manner the flesh could best be destroyed. At death the soul would be released from its prison of matter and would return to the Pleroma—a sort of world soul.

Gnosticism as a system was fairly short-lived, partly because of its inherent weaknesses and partly because the Polemicists (especially Irenaeus, Tertullian, and Hippolytus) were so effective in dealing with it. It left lasting effects on the church, however, negatively in promoting asceticism and division of Christians into higher and lower orders, and positively in forcing the church to come to a clearer definition of her doctrine and the limits of her canon. Gnosticism also helped to advance the institutionalization of the church in at least three ways. Its claim to be the universal church led the orthodox church to assert her claim to be the catholic church; its doctrinal inroads led to the rise of bishops as defenders of the faith; its emphasis on asceticism helped to foster the growth of monasticism in the church.

About the middle of the second century there arose in Phrygia (central Asia Minor) the Montanist error, so named for its leader, Montanus. Montanus taught that the end of the world was at hand and that he was introducing the Age of the Holy Spirit in preparation for the end of all things. He asserted that he was the manifestation of the Paraclete promised in John 14, and he claimed special revelations. The Montanists in general laid great emphasis on special spiritual gifts, and those of North Africa required a strict asceticism (involving fasting, celibacy, strict moral discipline, etc.) in view of the imminent end of the world. Montanism represented a reaction to the deadness and worldliness of the church, but its good effects were nullified by its extremes. Though generally orthodox, its emphasis on such spiritual gifts as continuance of prophetic revelation and its requirement of ascetic practices as if they were truths of revelation caused it to be condemned. The church declared that biblical revelation had come to an end and that special spiritual gifts were no longer operative.

During the third century three movements arose to challenge the authority and doctrinal solidarity of the church: Novatianism, Monarchianism, and Manicheism. Novatian was bishop of Rome, 251-253, and an able defender of the doctrine of the Trinity against the Monarchians. But he fell out with the hierarchy over the treatment of those who had renounced their faith in the face of Decius's persecution and later sought to renew their fellowship with the church. He denied the right of the church to restore the lapsed and advocated a purist concept of church membership that smacked of Montanistic legalism. The dissenting party chose him as bishop, and the result was a schism that spread over most of the Empire and lasted until the sixth century. In the fourth century, after the Diocletian persecution, the question of restoring the lapsed rose again; and a faction opposing restoration, known as the Donatists, emerged in North Africa. Subsequently, Novatian and Donatist groups seem to have merged.

Monarchianism (meaning "rule of one" and probably originating in Asia Minor) was more strictly a doctrinal error. The problem bothering the Monarchians was maintenance of the unity of the Godhead in the face of Trinitarianism. Their solution was something less than orthodox. Some of them, like the later Socinians and Unitarians, taught that the Father alone possessed true personality; the Son and Holy Spirit were merely impersonal attributes of the Godhead. So the power of God came upon the man Jesus and gradually penetrated and deified His humanity. But Jesus was not to be considered God in the truest sense of the word. Other Monarchians viewed the three persons of the Godhead as mere modes of expression or ways of describing God. They were not distinct, divine persons. This modalistic type of Monarchianism also came to be known as Sabellianism and Noetianism, after two of its leading exponents. The Monarchians called forth extensive and effective definition of the Trinitarian position. Although Monarchianism was dealt fatal body blows by the Polemicists, groups holding the Unitarian position have arisen repeatedly in Christendom.

Manicheism has been described as Gnosticism with its Christian elements reduced to a minimum and Oriental elements raised to a maximum. The system was developed by Mani in southern Babylonia about 240 and thereafter spread rapidly through Persia, India, China, Egypt, North Africa, and Italy. Its appeal was great, even claiming such leaders at St. Augustine among its adherents for a time. After a somewhat meteoric initial success, Manicheism rapidly lost ground and died out, probably in part because of the sterile rigidity that the system early attained.

Like Gnosticism, Manicheism was a dualistic system. The kingdom of darkness at one time attacked the kingdom of light, and the result was a mixed creation of light and darkness (good and evil) in which the kingdom of light is engaged in a program of gradual purification. Christ came into the world to aid the good principle in man to overcome the thrusts of the kingdom of darkness.

At the moment we are less concerned with the teaching of Manicheism than with its effects. In this system there were two classes: elect and auditors. Only the former were admitted to the secret rites of baptism and communion, which were celebrated with great pomp. The elect were very ascetic and occupied themselves with religious exercises. The auditors participated in the holiness of the elect in return for supplying the elect with the necessities of life. Manicheism helped to foster the ascetic spirit in the churches and was in large measure responsible for the division of church members into clergy and laity. Moreover, it promoted the growth of the priestly function, or the belief that ministers are intermediaries between God and man and have extraordinary power with God.

The effects of the perversions in the early church were both negative and positive. They introduced erroneous views and practices into the regular churches and hindered their growth and development. But they also forced church leaders to formulate more clearly the doctrines of the church and to establish the limits of the canon, which could furnish a source of truth for combating error.

In studying groups that have been branded heretical, one must be extremely careful. Frequently the only information about them that is still extant was produced by their enemies. Opponents commonly sought to portray them in the worst possible light. Therefore it is necessary to ask what sort of weakness their enemies would try to magnify and to figure out ways to evaluate the sources perceptively. The same sort of caution should be exercised in dealing with all minority positions in the history of the church, whether those persecuted by the medieval Inquisition, Anabaptists harried by the great Reformers, or New England revivalists opposed by the established churches during the Great Awakening. These and many others have been terribly misrepresented by those who were trying to shore up positions under severe attack.

4
Establishment of Canon and Creed

Books for a New Testament

Some think that the books to be included in the New Testament canon were decided on hastily, by a group of early church leaders, late on a hot summer afternoon. And it is sometimes implied that the choice of those men was no better than a comparable group of church officials would make in the twentieth century. The facts of history demonstrate, however, that the New Testament was not formed hastily, nor was it formed by the councils. It was the product of centuries of development, and its official ratification came in response to the practical needs of the churches.

Six main developments forced the church to formulate a canon of the New Testament. First, by the end of the first century contemporary witnesses to the message of Jesus and the apostles were mostly gone. The oral traditions became corrupt and conflicting, and believers wanted a body of Scripture that would spell out the authoritative message of the apostles. Second, from the beginning of the church it was customary to read Scripture in the worship services for the edification of believers.[1] Church leaders became increasingly concerned that the readings be truly the message of God for the people. Third, such heretics as Marcion[2] were formulating canons to promote their own special viewpoints. About A.D. 140 Marcion composed a canon of a mutilated Luke and ten of Paul's epistles. He rejected the Old Testament. In self-defense the church had to decide what books belonged in the canon.

Fourth, about the same time that Marcion and the Gnostics were making great inroads into the established churches, the Montanists began to promulgate ideas of continuing revelation. As noted in the last chapter, the church in retaliation declared that revelation had ceased. Fifth, obviously apocryphal works began to appear in increasing numbers. These gospels, acts, and epistles attempted to fill in gaps in the narrative of the life of Christ and the apostles and to round out the theological message of the church. Some of these books were obviously not on a par with the books we now recognize as canonical, but others were very close to the New Testament message. An effort needed to be made to separate the wheat from the chaff.

Last, the persecutions called for a decision on the contents of the New Testament canon. For instance the Diocletian persecution in 303 called for the burning of all sacred books and the punishment of those who possessed them. Preservation of Scripture in the face of such determined imperial opposition required great effort and endangered the lives of those who hid or copied it. Therefore one wanted to be sure he was expending effort or risking his life to disseminate or protect a genuine work.

We have been talking about the need for forming a canon, but have not yet defined what is meant by the term. The Greek word *kanōn* (rule or standard) designated the laws that governed the behavior society expected or the state demanded of its citizens.

1. At first readings were taken from the Old Testament only. Later they were chosen from the "Memoirs of the Apostles." The fact that Judaism had formed an Old Testament canon was important for establishing the principle of canonicity that would lead eventually to a New Testament canon.
2. Marcion was a native of Asia Minor; there his own father, a bishop, condemned him as a heretic. Thereafter, he went to Rome and established separatist congregations with views vaguely similar to those of the Gnostics.

Paul used the word in that sense in Galatians 6:16. By the middle of the second century, the terms *canon of truth* or *canon of faith* were applied to the creed of the church. The connection of the word with books of the New Testament seems to have originated with Athanasius about the middle of the fourth century. Later, in his *Festal Epistle*, written in 367, he spoke of the Scripture as "canonized" in contrast to the apocrypha. Thus the word came into church vocabulary, although the idea behind it had arisen in the earliest days of the church. Canonical Scripture, then, on the one hand provides a standard of doctrine and holy living and, on the other hand, meets the standard or tests of inspiration.

It is one thing to determine the need for a canon; it is quite another to decide what belongs in it. Tests of canonicity had to be employed. Early church Fathers suggested that those books were canonical that were inspired. But inspiration is rather intangible and subject to differences of opinion. So secondary tests were required. One of the most important of these was apostolicity: that is, was a book written by an apostle or someone very close to the apostles? Thus, Luke's gospel was accepted because of his close relationship with Paul; Mark's because of his close association with Peter and Paul. Of course Matthew and John were apostles. Then there was the test of internal appeal. Did a book contain moral or doctrinal elements that measured up to the standards set by the apostles in their acknowledged writings?

As these and other tests were applied in various ways over the centuries, the canon gradually developed. Conservatives have long held that all the New Testament books were written by about the end of the first century, in spite of liberal claims to the contrary. And archaeological evidence now quite effectively confirms the conservative position.[3] It seems that almost from the time of their composition, the four gospels and Acts were accepted as divinely inspired accounts of the life of Christ and the development of the early church. Various churches to which Paul

3. The trend is to increasingly earlier dates for composition of New Testament books, even in liberal circles. As an example of what is happening, the Anglican bishop John A. T. Robinson of Trinity College, Cambridge, has radically altered his previous position and has gone so far as to insist that all New Testament books were written between A.D. 47 and 70 (*Can We Trust the New Testament?* [Grand Rapids: Eerdmans, 1977], 63).

addressed his epistles accepted his word to them as coming from the mouth of God. And gradually nearby churches came to feel that letters sent to sister churches were of value for them too; so they made copies. In this way the Pauline epistles began to circulate individually and by the end of the second century as a collection. The story concerning the rest of the New Testament books is not so simple.

Testimony in the writings of the church Fathers to the existence and value of various New Testament books is extensive, beginning as early as the end of the first century with Clement of Rome. And there are other notable pieces of evidence. A full catalog of this information is quite out of the question; a few of the outstanding items are noted here. About the middle of the second century, Tatian composed the first harmony of the gospels. This wove together elements of the four gospels in such a way as to present a continuous narrative of the life of Christ. A decade or two later a canon was drawn up, now bearing the name Muratori, after the Italian scholar who published it. The work is not quite complete in the condition it has come to us. It apparently recognizes the four gospels, Acts, the Pauline epistles, Revelation, two (or three) epistles of John, and Jude. But it adds the Apocalypse of Peter and omits 1 and 2 Peter and Hebrews and possibly one of John's epistles.

From the time of Irenaeus (c. 175), the canon was thought to contain essentially the same books that appear in it today, though there were continuing disputes over some inclusions. The eminent Clement of Alexandria (c. 200) seemed to recognize all the New Testament books. His greater student, Origen (c. 250), divided the books into categories of universally accepted works and disputed works. In the former he put the four gospels, the thirteen epistles of Paul, 1 Peter, 1 John, Acts and Revelation. In the latter he put Hebrews, 2 Peter, 2 and 3 John, James, Jude, and four works not now part of the New Testament. He himself seems to have accepted nearly all the books now included in the New Testament.

Hebrews was disputed because its authorship was uncertain; 2 Peter, because it differed in style and vocabulary from 1 Peter; James and Jude, because they represented themselves as servants rather than apostles of Christ; 2 and 3 John because the author called himself an elder rather than an apostle. Eusebius, the great historian of the fourth century, also divided the New Testament books into accepted and disputed categories. In the former he listed the same ones as had Origen. He himself seemed to accept all those now included. Later in the century the great Jerome also accepted the present twenty-seven books and influenced the Synod of Rome (382) to take the same position. By the time of the Council of Carthage in 397 only the twenty-seven books we now accept were adopted as canonical. The same decision was rendered at Carthage in 419. But those were local councils; their decision was ratified at the ecumenical Council of Chalcedon in 451. Since that time there has been no continuing conflict on the subject.

Thus it can readily be seen that the story of the formation of the New Testament canon was a long one, not involving any hasty decision on the part of an ecclesiastical body. Basically, three steps were included in the process: divine inspiration, gradual human recognition and acceptance of the separate works, and official ratification or adoption of those books already universally accepted in the church.

Controversies and Creeds

Just as the New Testament canon developed in response to a need in the church, so did the creeds. In the days before the canon was formulated and when there were few copies of any of the New Testament books in circulation, believers required some standard to keep them in the path of truth. Moreover, they needed a standard by which to test heretical opinions. So very early, possibly near the end of the first century or beginning of the second, a rule of faith came into existence. Assuming different forms in different churches, it generally taught that Christ, the Son of God, suffered under Pontius Pilate, was crucified and died, was buried, rose again, and ascended into Heaven—for the remission of sins. This rule of faith, which has come to be called the Apostles' Creed, reached its present form about 750. In the early church, candidates for baptism often were asked if they assented to the various clauses of this standard of faith.

Other creeds were formulated too, in an effort to settle controversies that tore the church into opposing factions. Some of the controversies had to do with the nature of Christ, some with the Holy Spirit, and one with the nature of man. These doctrinal quarrels were handled very differently from those of the second and third centuries. When Christianity became a legal religion early in the fourth century, the emperor Constantine regarded himself as head of the Christian religion along with the other religions of state. Therefore when difficulties arose he called a church-wide or ecumenical council to deal with the matter and to formulate a statement (creed) of settlement. Other emperors followed the same practice. Although these struggles concerning Christ, the Holy Spirit, and man were going on concurrently, for the sake of clearer presentation they are separated here.

1. CONTROVERSIES CONCERNING THE NATURE OF CHRIST

About 318 Arius, an elder of Alexandria, found great difficulty in accepting the Trinitarian nature of the Godhead and began to teach that Christ was different in essence from the Father—that He was created by the Father and before that He did not exist. Athanasius, archdeacon of Alexandria, rose to meet the challenge, asserting that Christ and the Father were the same in essence and that the Son was eternal. His primary concern was that if Christ were a mere creature, faith in Him could not bring salvation to man. The controversy raged. The fact that a synod at Alexandria deposed Arius in 321 did not end the struggle. Arius was able to win over some of the leading churchmen of the East, and matters only grew worse. Finally Constantine felt obliged to step in and restore harmony. In 325 he called an ecumenical council at Nicea, in northwest Asia Minor. Over three hundred bishops and a number of lesser dignitaries gathered for the occasion. Ultimately the Althanasian party was able to carry the day, and the emperor himself was persuaded to throw his weight behind them. The creed drawn up declared that the Son was the same in essence with the Father, the only begotten of the Father, and very God of very God. But the troubles of the Athanasian party had only begun. In the seesawing fortunes of subsequent years Athanasius was banished by the emperor no less than five times, with the consequent periodic restoration of Arius. Gradually, however, the situation changed and the orthodox party came to enjoy a definite majority in the empire.

In the process of asserting the full deity of Christ, some theologians had done so at the expense of His humanity. They taught that a complete humanity could not be sinless and that the divine nature, while assuming a human body, took the place of the higher rational principle in man. Several synodical meetings condemned the idea of the defective humanity of Christ, and in 381 the ecumenical council of Constantinople finally asserted His true and full humanity.

Then a third issue arose. If Christ was both fully divine and fully human, how were the two natures related in one person? Nestorius, bishop of Constantinople, was one of those who saw the two natures in loose mechanical conjunction. Neither nature shared in the properties of the other; so the divine did not have a part in the sufferings of the human nature of Christ. It takes little effort to discover that this is not merely an academic question. As Cyril of Alexandria pointed out, if Nestorius were right, a sinner would be redeemed by the sufferings of a mere man, and a mere man could accomplish no redemption. The Nestorian controversy led to the calling of a third ecumenical council, at Ephesus in 431. The council met and anathematized the teachings of Nestorius before the Nestorian party arrived. When the outlawed party appeared, it set up a rival council. The emperor finally decided against the Nestorians, and Nestorius entered a monastery. The result of the council was to demonstrate that the majority of bishops were in favor of the doctrines of Cyril (who argued for a true union of the two natures), but clarification of the matter was left to a later council. Though the error called Nestorianism is correctly represented above, Nestorius argued that he himself did not hold such views. Possibly he was the victim of smear tactics and a power struggle in the early church.

Following the Council of Ephesus there was a great deal of dissatisfaction on the part of many. As has been pointed out, the Council of Ephesus was not a true meeting of minds in an effort to resolve issues. Moreover, Eutyches, abbot of a monastery near Constantinople, in an effort to demonstrate the true unity of the person of Christ, began to teach that after the incarnation of Christ the two natures fused into one so that the one nature partook of the properties of the other. Distinctions between the two natures were obliterated. His arguments heightened the controversy considerably. Again it should be pointed out that these are not mere academic issues. Complete confusion reigns if Eutyches was right. Omniscience is an attribute of Deity only; according to the flesh Christ grew in wisdom and stature and favor with God and men. Omnipresence is an attribute of Deity only; one of the important characteristics of a human body is that it is confined to a specific locality. If Christ is already physically omnipresent, how can He come a second time from heaven? At length a new general council was called at Chalcedon in 451. Its decision was that Christ was both truly God and truly man, and that the two natures were united in one Person without confusion, change, division, or separation.

Like the other councils discussed above, the Council of Chalcedon did not bring final settlement. In Palestine, Egypt, and Syria, groups arose to perpetuate the teachings of Cyril and Eutyches. They held out strongly for one nature in Christ. Ultimately they were able to force a fifth ecumenical council, the second at Constantinople, in 553, which ratified the Chalcedonian creed but made changes that tended to favor the Eutychians.

After the Second Constantinopolitan Council, another conflict arose over the person of Christ and concerned the issue of whether Christ had only one will. The supporters of this view held that if Christ had two wills, He would have sinned, because certainly the human will would have succumbed to temptation. Ultimately a council, the third at Constantinople, in 680-81, met to deal with this issue. The decision was to ratify the Chalcedonian Creed with the addition that Christ had two wills, the human and divine, the human will being subject to the divine.

While these great ecumenical councils did not settle for all time discussion concerning the nature of the person of Christ, they did set forth the chief elements that have characterized an orthodox Christology down through the ages: His true and full deity, His true and full humanity, and the true union of the two natures in one person, without fusion or confusion.

2. CONTROVERSIES CONCERNING THE HOLY SPIRIT

Reference has already been made to Montanist and Monarchian perversions of the doctrine of the Holy Spirit. And in connection with the Council of Nicea something has been said about Arius. A further word needs to be said here, however. Not only did Arius hold that Christ was different in essence from the Father; he also taught that the Holy Spirit was different in essence. In fact he seems to have believed that the Holy Spirit was the creature of a creature, that is, of Christ. Being particularly concerned with the nature of the person of Christ, the Nicene Council did not make detailed pronouncement about the Holy Spirit. It merely affirmed, "I believe in one Holy Spirit." But after the Nicene Council, further attacks of the Arian sort (known as Macedonianism because espoused by Macedonius) on the deity of the Holy Spirit brought forth an array of orthodox literature. The result was that at the First Council of Constantinople, in 381, the creed constructed had phrases asserting that the Holy Spirit was to be worshiped and glorified as was the Father, that He proceeded from the Father, and that He was responsible for revelation. In succeeding decades the doctrine of His deity was further defined; and in 451 the Council of Chalcedon made the declarations of the First Council of Constantinople more explicit.

3. CONTROVERSY CONCERNING MAN

The controversy concerning the nature of man was the only one that took place in the western part of the empire; all the rest took place in the East. Chief protagonists in the struggle were St. Augustine, bishop of Hippo in North Africa, and Pelagius, a British monk who ultimately found his way to North Africa. These men formed their views independently, not in reaction to one another.

Soon after arriving at Carthage, Pelagius clashed head on with the prevailing theological viewpoint; and the controversy spread rapidly to other provinces. Pelagius taught that Adam's sin affected only Adam; man, he said, was still born on the same plane as Adam. There was, therefore, no such thing as original sin. Sin involved an act of the will and was due to the bad example of Adam and society since Adam's time. God's grace was only relatively necessary; man could do right without such aid. Divine grace sought only to assist man, who chooses and acts in complete independence. Investigation has shown, however, that Pelagius was a man of personal piety and that he wanted to rely on Christ for forgiveness of sins.

Augustine on the other hand held to the unity of the race—that all had sinned in Adam. So men sinned because they were sinners and were so totally corrupted in their natures that they were unable to do good works that could achieve salvation. He viewed faith to believe as a gift from God. God elected some unto salvation; He simply passed by the nonelect. On occasion Augustine did, however, refer to some as predestined by God to everlasting damnation. He also spoke of the divine gift of perseverance in faith; so salvation was for him a work of God from start to finish. Unfortunately Augustine confused justification and sanctification; so justification was for him a process rather than a single act of God as taught in Paul's great epistle to the Romans.

Pelagius experienced considerable opposition almost as soon as he arrived in North Africa. He was condemned by a Carthaginian synod in 412, by Pope Innocent I in 416, by a general council of African churches in 418, and finally by the ecumenical council at Ephesus in 431.

But this did not mean the triumph of Augustinianism. Augustine was out of step with the church of his day. He stressed too much the inner Christian life and too little the external ceremonies; he denied that the Eucharist had any sin-atoning power apart from the faith of the partaker; although he advocated asceticism, he denied that it had any value apart from transformation of life into Christlikeness. He opposed the predominant sacramental method of achieving salvation. Unfortunately, his own statements about the value of baptism and his confusion between justification and sanctification contributed to the weakening of his legacy. So although Pelagianism was condemned, a sort of semi-Pelagianism was to win out—a system in which grace and human works were to join in achieving salvation, within the framework of the church and the sacramental system.

The years during which the first six great ecumenical councils met (325-681) were turbulent ones. They were years during which the church was torn asunder by theological controversy—controversy that produced great statements of faith. They were also years when the barbarians were chipping away at the borders of the Roman Empire, conquering the whole western portion of it. And they were years when the hierarchical church was developing its doctrine and organizational machinery. Let us now take a quick look at the rise and decline of the Roman church during the Middle Ages.

5

The Medieval Papacy

Beginnings

The Roman Catholic and Eastern Orthodox churches as they existed at the end of the Middle Ages and as they appear in the twentieth century are products of historical evolution. Though apologists for Roman Catholicism have been particularly adept at finding "biblical" precedents for new dogmas and organizational developments they have propounded, those with a less biased approach to history have not been similarly convinced.

In the New Testament the office of bishop is placed alongside those of the elder and deacon—whether equatable with that of elder it is not our purpose now to discuss. With Ignatius (about 110) arose an emphasis on obedience to the bishop. How many of the exhortations in his writings are genuine is debated; some are thought to be interpolations by later writers trying to bolster their points of view. In any case his heavy stress on obedience to bishops seems to be an indication that such subordination did not then exist. Moreover, there is no hint that by *bishop* Ignatius meant anything more than an overseer or pastor of a single congregation. He nowhere exhorted presbyters (elders) to obey bishops. Furthermore, he urged congregations on some occasions to obey presbyters and on others to obey deacons. Of paramount importance is the fact that in his writings obedience to bishops was urged to help prevent churches from being doctrinally torn apart—not to facilitate their normal functions.

By the end of the second century Irenaeus was asserting the unity of the church (a spiritual unity, not organic) by virtue of the headship of Christ and community of belief as handed down through a succession of elders. Thereafter a tendency arose to transform the spiritual unity into an organic unity. Irenaeus also taught that the Roman church had been established by Peter and Paul and that they had appointed successors. During following decades the distinction between presbyters and bishops became firmly established, and bishops with authority over the several individual churches of a large city became commonly accepted.

By the middle of the third century the influential Cyprian, bishop of Carthage, taught that the universal church (outside of which there was no salvation) was ruled by bishops who were the successors of the apostles. Apostolic authority, he held, was first given to Peter. So the church at Rome became predominant because Peter was believed to have founded it. Moreover, Cyprian asserted the priestly function of the clergy. Cyprian's *On the Unity of the Church* incorporates much of his thinking on the nature and government of the church.

By the time Christianity became a tolerated religion during Constantine's day (about A.D. 325), the concepts of the priestly function of the clergy, apostolic succession, the ruling bishop, and the recognition of the Roman bishop as first among equals were established. In 325 at the Council of Nicea, the bishops of Alexandria, Antioch, and Rome were given authority over divisions of the empire in which they were located. By the fifth century Rome was asserting that her primacy was intended in that arrangement. It remained for the Roman bishop to transform his primacy into supremacy.

There were several reasons why Rome could effectively compete against the others in her struggle for supremacy. First, she claimed Petrine foundation (actually a double apostolic foundation—Paul and Peter). Peter was chief of the apostles and the one, according to Rome, on whom the church was founded. And the dogma of apostolic succession, though it recognized that other bishops could trace their authority to other apostles, would grant prominence to Peter's successors. Second, the bishop of Rome was superior in the West, while bishops of Constantinople, Antioch, and Alexandria competed for supremacy within a relatively small area in the East. After Antioch and Alexandria fell to the Muslims in the seventh century, the only competition Rome faced was Constantinople.

Third, after the move of the capital from Rome to Constantinople in 330 political power in the West gradually declined. With the barbarian invasions and the chaos that ensued, the bishop of Rome became the most powerful figure there. He represented the only living institution, and the church took on civil functions. In Constantinople on the other hand, the continuing Roman Empire maintained itself through varying fortunes until 1453. There the bishop (patriarch) found himself subservient to the emperor and therefore less capable of asserting himself. In this connection it should be pointed out that when the power of the imperial government was weak, it was sometimes advantageous to the emperor to recognize the pretensions of Rome, in which case the bishop of Rome held virtual authority over the bishop of Constantinople. Finally, the church in the West was not constantly rent asunder by doctrinal controversy as was the church in the East. And in the midst of the controversies that did arise, the church at Rome always proved to be orthodox. So Rome was in a much stronger position to develop her program and extend her influence than were churches of the East.

In discussing the period of the beginnings of the Roman church (prior to the pivotal pontificate of Gregory I in 590), several important persons and developments should be mentioned. The formation of the canon and creeds has already been described, as has been the rise of errors and their effect on the development of Roman Catholic doctrine and practice. We have also noted the contributions of the church Fathers, especially those of Augustine, the great theologian, and Jerome, the translator of the Vulgate. But a few others require comment at this point.

The first of these is Leo I, bishop of Rome 440-461. He did much to advance the cause of the papacy. Taking advantage of disorder resulting from the Vandal conquest of the province of Africa, he managed to secure the recognition of his authority by the church there. He interfered in the affairs of the church in Gaul to the advantage of papal power, and he asserted his authority in Illyricum (Yugoslavia). By means of his statesmanship he saved Rome from being sacked by Attila the Hun in 452 and destroyed by Genseric the Vandal in 455; in the process, he added much to his prestige. And he obtained from emperor Valentinian III the declaration that bishops of Gaul and other Western provinces were to be subservient to the pope at Rome and that governors of provinces were to compel bishops to go to Rome when summoned by the pope.

Gelasius (bishop of Rome 492-496) instituted the claim of moral superintendence over political rulers on the part of the pope. While he recognized that there were two spheres of rule, the spiritual and the temporal, he claimed that the church must give account to God for the deeds of kings, and so the king must submit to the church in spiritual matters. Symmachus (bishop of Rome 498-514) added the dictum that no tribunal could compel the appearance of a pope or sentence him in his absence.

But of particular importance was the conversion of Clovis, a Frankish chieftain, in 496. Soon afterward, three thousand of his followers were baptized into the Roman church. The significance of Clovis's conversion can hardly be overestimated. It was momentous because it won for Clovis the support of the Roman Catholics in the West, where he was the only orthodox Roman Catholic prince. Ultimately he was able to conquer over half of modern France. Out of this beginning the empire of Charlemagne later emerged. Clovis's conversion was also significant because it meant that orthodox Christianity would win out in the West. Moreover, Frankish kings would protect or aid popes on various occasions in the future and would contribute to the establishment of the institutional church as it has become known in the medieval and modern worlds. Furthermore, his conversion was important because the medieval church was to a large degree the carrier of culture. The Roman Catholic church helped to preserve and modify the classical heritage that has been passed on to Europe and the Americas, and to a lesser degree to the entire world. Fortunately for the papacy this important conversion was supplemented by the decision of Recared, the Visigothic king of Spain, to abandon Arianism and become a Roman Catholic in 587. Henceforth orthodox Christianity maintained a foothold on the Iberian peninsula even after the Muslim conquest in 711-718.

As a direct or indirect result of the conversion of Clovis and Recared, Roman Catholicism ultimately was to become the virtually uncontested faith in most of the West and was to penetrate effectively elsewhere. All of Western Europe was to be organized into dioceses and parishes ruled over by the pope and the princes of the church. The totality of the populace was born into the Roman Catholic church, was baptized into the church, was married by the church, lived under the ministrations of the church, and was buried by the church. Throughout the Middle Ages western Europe never knew anything else. And as is true of any monopolistic power, conditions grew lax within the institutional church because of lack of competition to keep the church vibrant and effective. The form of religious establishment characteristic of mother countries was passed on to colonies with the advent of the modern era. Thus all of Latin America, the Philippines, and segments of Africa became Roman Catholic.

Gregory and His Successors

Gregory I, the Great (540-604), was one of the greatest leaders that the Roman church has ever had. Coming on the scene at a time of widespread political confusion with its consequent effects on the life and organization of the church, he became a stabilizing political influence and was largely responsible for the creation of the medieval papacy. Born into a noble, wealthy, and devout family, Gregory early turned to the monastic life as a way to glorify God. He spent his inherited fortune to found seven monasteries. For several years he represented the Roman bishop at Constantinople, and in 590 was elected bishop of Rome. Gregory never called himself pope, but he exercised all the power of later popes, maintaining more or less effective control over the churches of western Europe.

For many reasons Gregory was one of the most important popes in the history of Roman Catholicism. First, as noted above, he transformed the bishopric of Rome into a papal system that endured through the Middle Ages. Second, he introduced changes into the liturgy and sought the standardization of it. (Although Gregory was not responsible for the type of chant that bears his name, he did much to promulgate its use in worship services.) Third, from a theological standpoint, his system served as something of a converging point for lines of thought found in the councils and in the Fathers. Though Gregory's theology was not original, he is important for his definition of dogma and his incorporation of elements of the popular piety of his day into the official teachings of the Roman Catholic church. He put tradition on an equal basis with Scripture in determining dogma. Though he accepted the Augustinian view of original sin, he held that through baptism sin was forgiven and faith implanted so that an individual might work the works of God. For sins committed penance was required. He expanded the concept of purgatory and converted the Eucharist from a sacrament into a sacrifice for redemption, having value for the living and the dead. He officially approved the invocation of saints and martyrs and the use of relics and amulets to reduce temporal punishments. His view of Christ and the Trinity followed the decisions of the ecumenical councils.

Fourth, he was important for his writings. The *Moralia,* a commentary on Job, provided one of the patterns for the allegorical interpretation of Scripture common during the Middle Ages. His superstitious nature and that of the age is well displayed in his *Dialogues,* which concerns the lives and miracles of pious Fathers in Italy. And his *Pastoral Rule* was a practical work that instructed the bishop in the care of his flock and became a standard manual for the conduct of bishops. Gregory was a good preacher too, as evidenced by his forty sermons that have survived. Gregory's writings have earned for him a place among the four great Latin doctors of the Western church: Ambrose, Augustine, Jerome, Gregory. Fifth, Gregory promoted asceticism, especially as he enforced the celibacy of the clergy and as he restored monastic[1] discipline. Last, Gregory possessed great missionary zeal. He sent forty monks to England in 596 under the leadership of Augustine (not the famous bishop of Hippo, who died in 430). Their success was pronounced, especially in the area of Canterbury, which became the religious capital of England and the seat of the archbishop.

During the seventh century Gregory's successors hardly maintained the high place he had earned for them. More than one of them was condemned as a heretic. And it was a period when Roman monks in Britain were engaged in a struggle for supremacy with Irish monks who preceded them there.

For a long time Irish missionary activity had been extensive in Britain and Ireland. St. Patrick evangelized Ireland during the fifth century. Exactly when he went to Ireland is one of many unresolved questions concerning his ministry. What is clear from his autobiographical *Confession* and other meager information is that he was born in Britain, perhaps in a small town west of Glasgow, and that he was of Scottish parentage. He was snatched by pirates at the age of sixteen and forced to work as a slave in Ireland. After six years there, during which time he had a conversion experience, he escaped and returned to Britain and his family. Subsequently he had a night vision in which he received a call to evangelize Ireland. Presumably he received his training in Britain and subsequently became the greatest single force in the Christianization of Ireland. Evidently Patrick was biblical and evangelical in his preaching and his ministry, and the churches he founded were independent of Rome. So it may be concluded that he was neither Irish nor Roman Catholic.

On the foundation that Patrick laid, Finian of Clonard built the superstructure of Irish monasticism early in the sixth century.

---

1. Monasticism, with its ascetic approach to life, arose very early in the East, where its adherents generally lived a hermitic existence. Basil of Caesarea developed the movement on more of a community or communal basis during the fourth century, and about the same time the great Athanasius introduced it to the West. But it was St. Benedict (c. 500) who was responsible for the general monastic rule of poverty, chastity, and obedience and the type of monasticism that grew up in western Europe—a type that was more productive and practical than that of the East.

Learned Irish monks, filled with missionary zeal, ranged far and wide across Europe during the sixth and seventh centuries. St. Columba (d. 597) established the famous monastery on the island of Iona and became the apostle of Scotland. St. Columbanus (d. 615) ministered on the Continent, establishing monasteries in Gaul, Switzerland, and northern Italy. Other Irish monks went north to the Shetlands, the Hebrides, the Orkneys, and Iceland; south into England and east onto the Continent—along the Rhine, into Hungary and Italy.

A contest between free Irish Christianity and Roman Catholicism was inevitable. After a number of meetings between the Irish and Roman Catholics, King Oswy (Oswiu) of Northumbria (northeastern England) called a synod at Whitby in 663 to determine which group should be considered the official one. Roman Catholic spokesmen won him over, and Irish monks gradually withdrew northward. In 636 south Ireland had already submitted to the papacy, and in 697 north Ireland followed suit. Their home base within the fold of Roman Catholicism, the Irish lost much of their ability to establish new missions. But primitive British Christianity held out in the mountains of Wales and the highlands of Scotland and on offshore islands for a long time.

Meanwhile, far to the east a new and much greater threat was rising to challenge medieval Christianity. In 622 Mohammed made his famous move (*Hegira*) from Mecca to Medina, and thereafter began the successful period of his preaching. Constructing a theology that utilized elements of Judaism, Christianity, and Arabian heathenism, and infusing a fanatical zeal that brooked no opposition, he produced a steam roller movement that soon flattened the Middle East, North Africa, and part of Europe. In fact Islam has gained adherents until today it can claim about one-fifth of the world's population.

Although it is not the purpose of the present study to engage in theological discussion, Islam is so important in world history and culture that at least the five pillars that characterize the faithful should be noted: (1) accepting the creed, "There is no God but Allah, and Mohammed is his prophet"; (2) praying five times a day toward Mecca; (3) making a pilgrimage to Mecca at least once during one's lifetime; (4) giving alms for pious and charitable purposes; (5) fasting from sunrise to sunset throughout the sacred month of Ramadan. Often holy war is listed as a sixth pillar.

Several factors contributed to the rapid spread of Islam. (1) A positive, fanatical, monotheistic program that promised booty, positions of leadership, and salvation to those who would engage in world conquest was certainly a powerful incentive in obtaining followers. (2) The Roman Empire was rapidly decaying from within while it exhausted its resources and those of the Persian Empire as well in a grueling fight almost to the death. Neither the Persians nor the Byzantines[2] were any match for the fanatical Arabs. (3) The Byzantines alienated many of their provincials by extracting high taxes and excommunicating them for heretical religious views. (4) Many Semitic people of the Byzantine provinces actually had more in common with the Semitic Arab invaders than they did with their Byzantine (Greek) overlords. (5) The Muslims were not mere despoilers like the Huns. In the early days of the movement only non-Muslims paid taxes. Therefore it was to the advantage of the Muslims to maintain a prosperous economy in areas they conquered. Often they replaced only the top bureaucrats; most of the population remained relatively undisturbed. (6) Often Islam had superior generals. (7) The development of image worship in the Catholic church made the Christianity of the day look polytheistic to both the Muslims and many Catholics. Therefore Islam, with its monotheistic emphasis, seemed to be superior.

Before his death in 632 Mohammed had won much of western Arabia. His successor, Abu Bakr (632-634) rapidly conquered the rest of the peninsula and at the same time sent volunteers into Syria and Persia. Omar (634-644) began systematic conquest of the Roman provinces. In 635 he took Damascus. He completed conquest of Palestine in 640 and about the same time took most of the Persian Empire. Alexandria and most of Egypt surrendered in 640. Conquests continued rapidly under successive leaders. Between 685 and 705 the conquest of North Africa was completed, including the conversion of the Moors. In 711 the Muslims

2. Name applied to the eastern part of the Roman Empire, which became essentially Greek after the fall of the West to the barbarians.

invaded Spain and in seven years reached the borders of France. On they went. It seemed as if all Europe were doomed. Meanwhile, the advance continued into India.

At this point some abler popes came to the chair of St. Peter. And their efforts coincided with the continuing rise of the Frankish Kingdom and the efforts of great missionaries. The pontificate of Gregory II (715-731) was a time of especially great advance. Willibrord, a native of York in England, succeeded in planting the standards of the Roman church among the wild peoples of Holland and Denmark. Meanwhile Boniface (from Devonshire, England) became the great missionary of central Europe. He organized the church of Bavaria and later became archbishop of Mainz. With the support of Gregory II and Charles Martel, the real ruler of the Franks, he succeeded in reforming the Frankish churches, abolishing heathen customs, improving the morals of the priests, and systematizing church organization. Boniface brought the Frankish bishops to full support of Rome.

Back in Rome, Gregory was having his troubles. Leo the Isaurian, emperor at the time, sought to rid himself of the pope by violence, because Gregory opposed Leo's taxation policies in Italy and his interference with the church's use of images (to be discussed later). Supported by the people of Rome and the Lombards in northern Italy, Gregory managed to die a natural death.

Contemporary with Gregory II lived one of England's best known sons, the Venerable Bede, a monk who worked at the monasteries of Jarrow and Wearmouth in Northumbria. Though he wrote various biblical works (about forty in number), they are overshadowed by his *Ecclesiastical History of the English People*. This book provides much important detail concerning early English church history, and it earned for the author the title "Father of English history."

At the beginning of the rule of Gregory III (731-741), it looked as if Romanism were doomed in Western Europe. The Lombards had got out of hand and threatened to destroy the church in Italy. But the greater danger was posed by the Muslims, who were advancing steadily north into France. Charles Martel, not actual king of the Franks, but mayor of the palace, summoned enough force to defeat the Muslims near Tours in central France in 732.

This victory threw the Moors back into Spain and made Charles the defender and leader of Western Christendom. Charles Martel also came to the aid of the pope in his struggle with the Lombards. Negotiations began during these years for an alliance between the Franks and the papacy. And the next half century was characterized by increasing cooperation between the king and the pope, the king often coming to the aid of the pope. In fact, Pope Zacharias recognized Pepin, son of Charles Martel, as king of the Franks in 751 in return for Pepin's military aid. To make the transfer of kingship from the line of Clovis official, Pope Stephen II came to Gaul in 754 to crown Pepin king of the Franks. All this was a foreshadowing of the time when the pope would anoint Charlemagne.

Church-State Alliance

The year 800 serves as a pivotal date in history. On Christmas day in Rome, Pope Leo III crowned Charlemagne "emperor of the Romans." Charlemagne seems to have interpreted this to mean that he was the leader of Western Christendom, the monarch of a new "Christian empire," rather than the inheritor of the old Roman imperial office. His son Louis the Pious and successive kings in the line made more of Roman imperial ideals. Hence there came into being the concept of a Holy Roman Empire. This empire was called Roman because it was to succeed the now defunct power of Rome in the West. It was called holy because it was to be supreme over Christendom. This new arrangement constituted an alliance of sorts between the pope and the emperor, according to which each was to have dominion within his own sphere and each was to cooperate with the other and promote the interests of the other. But as a matter of fact, during succeeding generations popes and emperors engaged in periodic struggles to see who could dominate the other. Beyond the immediate significance, the concept of the Holy Roman Empire was to have some long-range effects on European history. For a thousand years one European ruler or another tore up the countryside with his armies in an effort to establish himself as successor of the Caesars. Finally, Napoleon abolished the empire in 1806.

By inheritance and force of arms, Charlemagne won control of a vast chunk of Western Europe—it stretched from the Atlantic eastward to the Elbe and Danube rivers and from the North Sea to the Mediterranean and included much of Italy and a little of Spain. In the process he maintained rather effective control of the pope and the Roman church. His capitularies, or laws, had to do with both church and secular affairs. Not only did he regulate the lives of the clergy, but he also directed that bishops and abbots should set up schools. Charlemagne's son Louis was not so capable; and his grandsons split the empire three ways in the Treaty of Verdun in 843. According to that arrangement, Charles took the area roughly encompassing that of modern France; Louis, modern Germany; and Lothair, a strip of territory extending from the lowlands into northern Italy.

Thereafter the process of political disintegration went forward rapidly. The territory of Lothair suffered encroachment by the other two descendants of Charlemagne. With the death of Charles III (the Fat) in 887, the Carolingian line came to an end in Germany; at the same time the Carolingian empire as any sort of unit also came to an end. After a time of confusion Otto I was crowned king of the East Franks in 936 and introduced the Saxon line. Carolingians continued to rule weakly in France until 987, when the line of Hugh Capet rose to the kingship. Henceforth the Holy Roman Empire was essentially a German entity, with a king elected by and checkmated by a number of powerful nobles. In reality, under feudalism it was divided into a host of small antagonistic principalities.

While political disintegration occurred internally in the empire, external attacks multiplied. During the ninth century Vikings terrorized the northwest and western parts of the empire, Muslims ravaged Sardinia and Corsica and the coasts of southern France and western Italy, and the Magyars (from Russia) raided the eastern borders of the Christian lands and settled down in the area now known as Hungary. Slavs and Bulgars also attacked in the eastern parts just prior to incursions of the Magyars.

It is purposed to include under this heading of Church-State Alliance the whole period from 800 to 1073. The papacy reached a high point of development when allied with Charlemagne, but it declined with the fortunes of his house and the political disintegration of Europe.

By the time of Pope John VIII (872-82), the Carolingian line was about to expire. Muslim pirates ranged all along the Italian coast and threatened Rome itself. Though the emperor tried to help John, he had little strength left. The pope himself was forced to raise a fleet and do battle with the Muslims to save the Italian coast. To keep them out of Rome, he had to agree to pay annual tribute. During much of the period between 880 and 1000, Italy was in anarchy, and the papacy suffered accordingly. For instance, there were twelve popes between 882 and 904. Wealthy families sometimes bought their way into the papacy. Military and political forces were exerted on the choice and conduct of popes. The chair of St. Peter was occupied by some very unworthy individuals between about 880 and 1060. For example, near the end of the period Benedict IX was pope. Even such a nonsectarian source as the *Encyclopaedia Britannica* notes that he became pope at twelve, was guilty of gross disorders of conduct, and was driven out of Rome by the local population more than once because of his disorderly conduct. But nothing is served by portraying the papacy at its worst. As a matter of fact, it is amazing that so many popes of the period were quite capable and that the church advanced considerably under such handicaps.

Surprisingly enough, the boundaries of Christendom greatly increased between 800 and 1073. Before the middle of the ninth century an archbishopric was established at Hamburg, and around the same time Roman Catholicism claimed Bohemia and Moravia. Approximately a century later it was officially adopted in Poland. About 1000, Olaf I made it the faith of Norway; and shortly thereafter Norwegian missionaries won Iceland to Christianity. About the same time, Leif the Lucky evangelized Greenland, the Swedish King Olaf established Roman Catholicism as the faith of Sweden, and Canute the Great completed the Christianization of Denmark. Concurrently, King Stephen I (St. Stephen) effectively established the church in Hungary.

Meanwhile Eastern Christians were evangelizing to the north of Constantinople. Cyril and Methodius were successful in Bulgaria during the ninth century, and King Boris made it the official faith of the realm. During the tenth and eleventh centuries Russia was won over. Following the baptism of King Vladimir in 988 the Eastern Slavs as one body turned to Christianity—just as the Franks had at the baptism of Clovis.

Not only did the Roman church greatly extend her territory from 800 to 1073, she also greatly extended her power. With the political fragmentation of Europe, the pope often stood a better chance of bringing princes, particularly the lesser ones, to terms. As Christianity spread and with it the idea that salvation came only through membership in the church, the threat of excommunication was often enough to bring rulers to terms. If it was not, the papacy could try interdict—withholding services of the church from the people of a whole area. In such cases the populace usually brought enough pressure on the king or noble to insure a victory for the pope.

One more development needs to be considered before going on to view the medieval papacy at its height: the split between the Eastern Orthodox and Roman Catholic churches. Several factors were responsible for the split. The first of these was the iconoclastic controversy: the controversy over the use of images. Leo the Isaurian, the Byzantine emperor, issued the first decree against their use in 726—in part to meet the Muslim charge that Christianity was polytheistic. He was supported by the patriarch of Constantinople and the higher clergy but was opposed by many of the monks and the common people. Gregory II, at Rome, denounced Leo's edict—both because the problem hardly existed in the West and because Rome held that political power had no right to interfere in the affairs of the church. The controversy produced a definite breach between Rome and Constantinople. Gregory III was the last pope to seek confirmation of his election from Constantinople, and in 781 the popes ceased mentioning the name of the emperor in dating their documents. Their ties to the East cut, the popes henceforth turned to the Franks for aid; thus the Franco-papal alliance was an important result of the iconoclastic controversy. It was not until 843 that a church council in the East finally settled the matter in favor of the use of images (but only pictures, not statues); by that time the damage to unity had been done.

The second factor was the conflict over the procession of the Holy Spirit, known as the Filioque Controversy. The East taught that the Holy Spirit proceeded from the Father alone; the West, believing that such a view did not give proper recognition to the Son, asserted that He proceeded from the Father and the Son (*Filioque* means *and the son*). Third, the patriarch of Constantinople and the pope at Rome were unwilling to be subservient to each other. Fourth, there was no sharp definition of the boundaries between territories to be ruled by Rome and Constantinople, and frequent struggles arose over administration of border areas. Fifth, basic differences in cultural background and influence between East and West hindered understanding and cooperation. Sixth, in the East the church was subservient to the emperor; the church in the West insisted on independence from the state and demanded the church's right of moral superintendence over rulers of state. Seventh, there were numerous liturgical differences between the two churches (e.g., whether leavened or unleavened bread was to be used in the Eucharist), as well as a host of other minor variations (e.g., whether clergy were to be bearded or clean shaven). Debates continued between the two bodies; finally, in 1054, a Roman delegation laid the bull of excommunication on the altar of St. Sophia in Constantinople. Of course the Greek patriarch retaliated. Thus the schism was complete.

The Medieval Papacy at Its Height

A new chapter in papal history began in 1073, when Hildebrand assumed the chair of St. Peter under the name of Gregory VII. His program and philosophy were basic to the achievement of supremacy in Christendom attained by the popes of the thirteenth century. For some twenty years before he became pope, Hildebrand was a power behind the papal throne. During that time Nicholas II, with Hildebrand's support, succeeded in reforming papal election procedure. Formerly popes were selected by the seven deacons of Rome, aristocratic faction of the populace, and German emperors. Henceforth they were to be elected by the college of cardinals, a procedure that is still in effect.

However, Hildebrand was acclaimed by the crowd at the funeral of Alexander II and carried to St. Peter's in Chains and crowned pope.

As pontiff, Gregory held to the supremacy of the pope within the church and over temporal rulers. He carried on an unrelenting program to reduce all bishops, abbots, and clergy to absolute subjection to the papacy and was quite successful. He saw three particular abuses that needed correcting: the marriage of the clergy (or clerical concubinage), simony, and investiture by secular princes. Gregory issued a ban on clerical marriage in 1074 and thereby prevented the clergy from becoming a hereditary caste; instead they were to become loyal to the pope. On simony (the buying or selling of church offices) he made unrelenting warfare and was reasonably successful. The problem of lay investiture was another story.

When a bishop or abbot or other high church official was appointed, he was supposed to receive investiture with spiritual authority by his ecclesiastical superior and investiture with temporal authority by the secular lord of the area where he was to serve. For centuries the political leaders of Europe had been accustomed to appointing and/or investing with spiritual and secular authority the higher clergy of their realms. Understandably, such a practice often did not result in appointments of clerical leaders who were either spiritually sensitive or loyal to the church. The reforming efforts of Gregory VII could only touch off a fight.

His great test of strength arose over the choice of the archbishop of Milan. Gregory's opponent was Henry IV, emperor of the Holy Roman Empire; both emperor and pope had a candidate for office. Henry was at a disadvantage because he was also engaged in an internal power struggle with some of the Saxon nobles. Gregory threatened excommunication if Henry IV did not comply; Henry answered with a council at Worms (1076), which rejected papal authority. Henry was excommunicated and his subjects were absolved of allegiance to him. The German nobles then demanded that Henry achieve reconciliation with Gregory within a year or forfeit his throne. So Henry was forced to make his peace with Gregory. But in the ensuing years Henry won the last round; he marched on Rome and set up a pope of his own choice, and Gregory died in exile.

In the days of Henry's son Henry V, the papacy ultimately won the investiture struggle, however. At Worms in 1122 a concordat was drawn up according to which the emperor consented to permit the church to elect bishops and abbots and invest them with spiritual power. Although elections were to be held in the presence of the king, he could not use simony or violence. Elected officials of the church were to pledge allegiance to the temporal power.

THE CRUSADES

In part, the call for a crusade must be viewed as connected with the investiture struggle. At the Council of Clermont in 1095, in the midst of a contest with Henry IV, Urban II proclaimed a Crusade. This was evidently a show of force in his struggle with the emperor. By this means Rome could direct the energies of Europe in a way that would bring her great advantages. Although many went on the Crusades for economic reasons, or for adventure, or for other lesser reasons, the primary and official motive of the Crusades was religious. In fact Urban promised remission of sins to those who marched under the banner of the cross. The event that sparked the Crusades was the advance of the Seljuk Turks in the East and the call for help from the Byzantine emperor Alexius I. Tales of the sufferings pilgrims endured at the hands of the Turks in the Holy Land provided emotional appeal for many to engage in holy war.

In response to Urban's call a great host gathered from Western Europe, especially from France, the Lowlands, and Italy, and finally took Jerusalem in 1099. The Crusaders then set up the kingdom of Jerusalem. Estimates of the number participating in this Crusade range from fifty thousand to six hundred thousand. One must be careful about dogmatically following any statistician, but the number of fighting men was only a few thousand.

The burden of arousing enthusiasm for the Second Crusade (1147) fell on the famous Bernard of Clairvaux. Europeans were concerned with meeting the Muslim threat to the northern borders of the kingdom of Jerusalem. The king of France and the emperor of the Holy Roman Empire led the Crusade, but it was completely unsuccessful, leaving Jerusalem in greater danger than before. The crusading movement ground to a standstill until 1187, when Jerusalem was captured by Saladin and all Christendom was again aroused.

The Third Crusade (1189-92) is known as the Crusade of the Three Kings: Richard I of England, Philip Augustus of France, and Frederick I of Germany. Frederick drowned on the way to Palestine; Philip stayed in Palestine for only a very short time, leaving Richard to carry on the struggle alone. Although he was unsuccessful in taking Jerusalem, he did win permission for pilgrims to enter the Holy City for a few years.

The Fourth Crusade began in 1201 under the leadership of Pope Innocent III. He urged the capture of Egypt as a base of operations against Palestine. When the army gathered, it found itself without sufficient funds to pay for shipping. In return for financial guarantees it agreed with Venice to recapture nearby Zara from the Hungarians. For the same reason, it subsequently decided to support the deposed Byzantine emperor in his bid to regain the throne of the empire. The attack on Byzantium was more fiercely opposed than the Crusaders had expected, however. The result was a prolonged struggle there, permanent sidetracking of the Crusade, destruction of the power of the Eastern empire, and establishment of a Latin kingdom in its place. Innocent was able to have some indirect influence in this Latin kingdom and over the Eastern Orthodox church until 1261, when the Eastern empire regained her independence.

The last Crusades of any significance was the sixth, led by Frederick II of Germany in 1228-29. By diplomacy he acquired for fifteen years Jerusalem, Bethlehem, Nazareth, and a corridor connecting Acre and Jerusalem.

The Crusades ended in failure, with Jerusalem falling to the Egyptians in 1244 and remaining in Muslim hands until 1917, when General Allenby captured the Holy City from the Turks. Yet is must be said that while the Crusades lasted, the Roman church enjoyed wave after wave of popular enthusiasm in support of her causes. Moreover, while the church directed the energies of Europeans in fighting an external foe, she provided a safety valve that spared her a great deal of internal stress.

The effects of the Crusades were destined to be mainly political, social, and economic rather than religious. They contributed to the commercial revolution and its accompanying rise of the middle class, the demise of feudalism, and the decline of provincialism in Western Europe. It is hard to measure fully the impact on Western Europe of the travel of hundreds of thousands of people to strange lands where they discovered new foods, new modes of dress, and new ways of doing things.

INNOCENT III

Directing the affairs of the medieval papacy at the very height of her power was Innocent III (1198-1216). As has already been noted, he had some indirect influence over the Eastern church and empire. In Western Europe, he forced his will on France, England, and the Holy Roman Empire. He humiliated Philip Augustus of France, forcing him to take back his divorced wife, who had appealed to the pope. Innocent did this by laying an interdict on the whole nation of France. Shortly thereafter he humbled King John of England in a struggle over the appointment of a new archbishop of Canterbury. Again Innocent used the method of interdict, as well as inviting Philip of France to invade England if John refused to come to terms. About the same time, Innocent interfered in the affairs of Germany, dictating the imperial succession there. Again he used a threat of French troops to accomplish his aim. Last, Innocent called the Fourth Lateran Council (1215) to settle certain doctrinal matters. It decided that annual confession to a priest was mandatory for all laymen. And it enunciated the dogma of transubstantiation, which means that the bread and wine become the actual body and blood of Christ upon pronouncement of the priest. The priest could then perform an actual sacrifice of Christ every time the mass was said. Moreover, the council gave official sanction to the seven sacraments and provided some definition of them.

THE INQUISITION

One of the strengths of the medieval papacy in maintaining her power over the populace of Western Europe was the Inquisition. In the process of development for a couple of centuries, the medieval Inquisition came to its definitive formulation under Pope Gregory IX (1227-41). It was designed to inquire into the spread of heresy and to call before its tribunals Roman Catholics suspected of heresy in order to secure their repentance. The program was launched merely to keep the faithful in line, not to obtain the conversion of Jews and Muslims. The great purges against those peoples in Spain were inventions of the Spanish throne. The Inquisition was deemed a necessity because of the spread of groups such as the Waldenses (discussed in chap. 6), which, if allowed to go unchecked, threatened the very life of the papacy.

Generally, the Dominicans were in charge of Inquisitorial activities. Trials were held in secret. There was no way of obtaining legal defense, because any lawyer representing an accused person would himself become the target of church tribunals. Confessions might be extracted by torture, and testimony against the accused might be obtained from witnesses by the same means. Those who confessed and were reconciled might be subjected to various punishments, including penances, pilgrimages, scourgings, or fines. Those who refused to recant commonly were imprisoned for life or handed over to the secular authorities to be executed, usually by burning. The excesses of the Inquisition (sometimes called an engine of iniquity), its violation of human rights, and in some places its reign of terror must forever remain as a blot on the history of the Roman church.

SCHOLASTICISM

It has already been noted that at the height of her power the medieval papacy defined the dogma of transubstantiation and declared the necessity of annual confession to a priest. Other dogmas and doctrines were being formulated at this time too, largely through the efforts of the Scholastics. Scholasticism is hard to define adequately, but certain generalizations may be made concerning it. It was the sum of the teachings and methods of the prominent Western philosophers most widely accepted during the Middle Ages. It constituted a harmonization of philosophy and theology in one system for the purpose of rational demonstration of theological truth. The Scholastics sought certainty of the truth and salvation by way of knowledge and reason. The ninth to the twelfth centuries mark the formative period of Scholasticism, the thirteenth century the height, and the fourteenth and fifteenth centuries a period of decline. Anselm and Abelard are usually thought of as cofounders; Hugo and Peter Lombard as important representatives along the way; Thomas Aquinas as representing the movement at its height; and Duns Scotus and William of Ockam as typical writers during the decline.

The Scholastics, and especially Aquinas, are responsible for helping to formulate the sacramental system of the Roman church—a system through which one was to obtain salvation. They pegged the number of sacraments at seven, and then spelled out in greater detail the significance of baptism, the Eucharist, confirmation, penance, extreme unction, holy orders, and marriage. Also, they set forth theories of the atonement still common today, defined the way of salvation, and in general produced many of the ideas that the Council of Trent (1545-1563) would draw together in a tight, coherent system and would officially establish as orthodox Roman Catholic teaching for centuries to come.

MYSTICISM

Contemporary with the Scholastic movement came mysticism, which aimed at a certainty of salvation and the truth through spiritual experience. Some of the mystics went to great excess in their emphasis on a love experience with God, but many of them seem to have been genuine believers. Three of the better mystics—all of the twelfth century—were Richard and Hugh of St. Victor and Bernard of Clairvaux. The latter is known for the famous hymns attributed to him, "Jesus the Very Thought of Thee" and "O Sacred Head, Now Wounded." One way that mystics sought to experience Christ was by walking where He walked and suffering where He suffered. Thus participating in a Crusade was a natural outgrowth of their religious orientation. It is no accident that Bernard of Clairvaux, one of the best-known mystics, was a leader of the Second Crusade. Mysticism and Scholasticism were a good counterbalance for each other. Mysticism kept Scholasticism from being too academic, and Scholasticism helped the mystics keep their feet on the ground.

MONASTICISM

In a very real sense the backbone of the medieval papacy was the monastic movement. Long is the roll of great leaders of the Middle Ages who came from the monastery. It includes such famous names as Gregory I and VII, Richard and Hugh of St. Victor, and Bernard of Clairvaux. The monasteries were the conservatories of learning and the centers of missionary and philanthropic work. The monks were the writers, preachers, philosophers, and theologians of the age; they headed the Inquisition and persuaded multitudes to participate in the Crusades. And it may be said that the monasteries provided something of a safety valve for the Roman church, for in them earnest Christians had a great deal more freedom from ecclesiastical machinery than they would have had outside the cloister. Without this freedom, it is possible that much of the evangelical life would have parted company with Romanism sooner than it did. It should be remembered that Luther, Erasmus, and many other critics of the papacy had monastic backgrounds.

St. Benedict (about 500) developed the Western European form of monastic life, and other orders were, in general, offshoots of the Benedictine order. The Cluniac order came into being in 910, the Cistercian in 1098. The latter's most illustrious son was Bernard of Clairvaux. St. Francis of Assisi founded the Franciscan order in 1210, and St. Dominic founded the Dominicans in 1215. The Augustinian order was formed out of a number of older bodies in 1244. The thirteenth century was the heyday of monasticism. It declined at the end of that century and throughout the fourteenth. There was some reform in the fifteenth century. The Reformation destroyed most of the monasteries of northern Europe and seriously curtailed the activities of those in central Europe.

Decline of the Medieval Church

The period of the decline of the medieval church may be dated between 1305 and 1517. The first date marks the beginning of the Babylonian Captivity of the papacy, which is discussed below; the latter is the year Luther posted his theses on the church door at Wittenberg.

There were many reasons for the decline of the papacy. First, there were the rise of national monarchs and the decline of feudalism; correspondingly, there was a developing sense of nationality and increased loyalty of the people to their rulers. The church claimed a supranational loyalty, which would certainly suffer with the spread of the new intense nationalism. As strong monarchs arose they became jealous of the immense wealth and power that the church held within their monarchal borders. Second, the rigid enforcement of doctrine and practice, especially by means of the Inquisition, stirred up opposition and dissent. Third, the increasing cost of maintaining the hierarchy and the employment of oppressive means of securing money alienated many. Fourth, there was an increasing moral laxity among churchmen, especially in the fifteenth century.

Fifth, the moral relaxation was accompanied by a general secularization of the church during the fourteenth and especially the fifteenth centuries. Secularization of all of life was in process, a feature of the Renaissance. The Renaissance was not just a rebirth of knowledge; it was a rebirth of the classical spirit, with its rationalistic outlook on life. The classical world had formulated its ethics by means of philosophy and therefore found them to be relativistic; it did not follow an unchangeable revealed standard. Moreover, the Renaissance marked the rise of the middle class with new wealth, commonly spent on art, literature, education, and the like, rather than on the church. Spurred by the thought patterns of the classical world and an improved economic climate, men of the Renaissance subscribed to a humanistic orientation to life. Man instead of God increasingly became the measure of all things. There was a desire to make this world a more fit place for human beings instead of concentrating all efforts on preparing for the life hereafter. The heady individualistic spirit of the Renaissance also weakened the corporate orientation and demands of the Roman church. An important phenomenon of the Renaissance was the invention of printing, which facilitated not only the distribution of Scripture and a return to New Testament Christianity, but also the spread of satirical or critical writings that often ridiculed the church.

Sixth, the Crusades contributed in many ways to the decline of the church. For example, hordes of Europeans who had lived within sight of their lord's manor house, without education, bred on superstitions of the times, learned that life elsewhere was different. The new ideas and ways of life with which they came in contact in the East weakened the ties of many to the church. Last, the Babylonian Captivity of the church and the Papal Schism did much to weaken the power of Rome in Western Europe.

The Babylonian Captivity was a period of approximately seventy years (1305-1377) when the pope ruled from Avignon, just outside the southern border of France. It was called the Babylonian Captivity by ardent Roman Catholics of a later time because they likened this period when the pope presumably was a virtual prisoner of the French king to the seventy years when the Hebrews were captive in Babylonia.

The captivity came about partly because of rising nationalism and partly because Pope Boniface VIII overreached himself. Boniface, in his famous bull *Unam Sanctam* (1302), insisted that all rulers were subject to him and that it was "necessary for salvation" for every human being to be subject to the pope. Philip IV of France, who was having a running battle with Boniface, sent representatives to Italy to arrest the pope. Rescued by the townspeople at his home at Anagni, Italy, Boniface died a month later. His successor, Benedict XI (1303-1304), lasted for only eight stormy months, and the papal chair remained vacant for eleven months thereafter. Finally it was filled by Clement V, a French churchman chosen by King Philip. Trying to remove himself from the direct presence of the French king and afraid to face the Italian people, Clement settled down at Avignon in 1309.

Whether or not later popes were under French control, Clement was, and all popes of the period were Frenchmen. Political rulers of the later part of the captivity seemed to feel that papal interests were closely identified with those of France. Such a belief was bound to have significant effects. For example, during the Babylonian Captivity the Hundred Years War broke out between France and England, greatly weakening the power of the papacy in England. During the war, the pope demanded the surrender of Wycliffe, the great reformer; but a powerful party at the English court protected him. Furthermore, the papacy gained a reputation for extravagance in expenditure and offensiveness in taxation during this period.

The Papal Schism (1378-1417) hurt the papacy even more than the Babylonian Captivity. The schism resulted from the total incompetence of Pope Urban VI, who within a few months of his election in Rome (1378) had alienated the entire college of cardinals. Ultimately all the French cardinals slipped out of Rome, declared Urban's election void, and elevated Robert of Geneva to the papacy as Clement VII. When Urban refused to be deposed, the French cardinals and Clement moved to Avignon and the rupture was complete. Naturally, the princes of Europe lined up behind the pope of their choice, and Christendom was split. When the Council of Pisa (1409) tried to settle the problem by deposing the two existing popes and installing a single one in their place, all it succeeded in doing was electing a third pope; so for several years there were three popes anathematizing and excommunicating one another. Christendom was utterly confused, and reforming parties grew rapidly. It must be remembered that during this period Hus preached with great success in Bohemia, and the Lollards (followers of Wycliffe) secured a large following in England and Scotland. Finally the Council of Constance managed to depose all three popes in 1417 and elect a new one, who henceforth would permanently reside in Rome.

Some have called the last part of the fifteenth century the paganized stage of the papacy. The Renaissance was taking its toll in the secularization of some of the top clergy. Pope Nicholas V

(1447-1455) was a great lover of classical literature and the founder of the Vatican library. He spent considerable sums on his pet project and on the repair of numerous classical structures in Rome. Julius II (1503-1513) is known as the patron of artists, especially Michelangelo, who painted the Sistine Chapel ceiling from 1508 to 1512. And Leo X (1513-1521), pope when the Reformation began, was very extravagant. His court life was a constant round of banquets, theatrical shows, and balls. As builder of St. Peter's in Rome, he used the revenues of the papacy on art, architecture, and the like. It should be remembered that his conflict with Luther came over the sale of indulgences—designed to raise money for the building of St. Peter's.

So at the beginning of the sixteenth century the medieval papacy was sick. Some within the system began to make prescriptions for cure of the illness. These, coupled with the disruption brought about by the Reformers, stirred the church to make changes that permitted a strong resurgence of power in later years.

6

Disruption of the Holy Catholic Church

Long before Luther fired his verbal salvo against indulgences and launched the Reformation, others had sniped at the theological position of the Roman Catholic church. In fact, there always had been those within the Roman church who did not agree with its teaching, and many had even broken away into separate religious communities.

Forerunners of the Reformation

Peter Waldo, one of the most effective of the pre-Lutheran Reformers, was a wealthy merchant of Lyons, France. Impressed with the way of poverty and service to Christ as the path to heaven (based on Matthew 19:21), he sold most of his holdings in 1176 and gave the proceeds to the poor. He retained some property to care for his wife and daughters, however. Within a year or so, he was joined by others, men and women, who called themselves the "Poor in Spirit," and undertook an itinerant ministry of preaching repentance and living from the handouts of listeners. As good Roman Catholics, they appealed to the Third Lateran Council in 1179 for permission to preach but were refused because they were thought to be ignorant laymen. Convinced

75

that they, like early believers, should obey God rather than men, Peter and his followers continued to preach. In 1184, Pope Lucius III excommunicated them for their disobedience. This act brought them numerous supporters, and the movement spread into southern France, Italy, Spain, the Rhine Valley, and Bohemia. It is hard to know whether all the individuals classified as Waldenses were part of the movement or whether contemporary Roman Catholic opponents merely used the term as a blanket descriptive for many disaffected individuals who opposed the official church.

At any rate the true Waldenses seem to have taken the New Testament as a rule of faith and life and appear to have used it in a rather legalistic sense. They went about two by two, wearing simple clothing, preaching repentance, engaging in frequent fasting, and living from the gifts of others. They rejected purgatory and masses and prayers for the dead and held to the necessity of using vernacular translations of Scripture. They insisted on the right of both laymen and laywomen to preach, but they did have an organization with bishops, priests, and deacons. Perhaps it should be noted that Waldo (also Valdez, or Valdes) seems never to have become fully evangelical in the best sense of the term. But in pointing to the Scripture as the source of religious truth, he opened the door for his followers to become truly evangelical.

The Waldenses were severely persecuted for centuries. Part of the reason for their widespread distribution in Europe was that they were driven from their homeland. In Bohemia they ultimately became part of the Hussite movement. In the mountain fastnesses of the Cottian Alps between France and Italy, their real homeland by the time of the Reformation, they met in historic conclave with representatives of the Genevan Reformation in 1532 and adopted the theology and government of the Swiss Reformers. Subsequently, in 1545, some three to four thousand of them were massacred in Provence (France). Finally, in 1848, they won toleration in the kingdom of Sardinia and subsequently in a united Italy. They are the only late medieval separatist group to survive to the present, though of course numerous changes in organization and teaching have taken place among them.

John Wycliffe. Like Peter Waldo, John Wycliffe (1320?-1384) was a biblical reformer, bringing to bear the teachings of Scripture on the practices of the Roman church. He also engaged in Bible translation, and it was largely through his efforts that the first English version was produced. Though he personally translated or supervised translation of much of the Bible, his version was not completed until after his death, by Nicholas of Hereford and John Purvey. Without doubt its widespread use had an influence on the development of the English language. Descended from a noble family, Wycliffe was educated at Oxford and later became master of Balliol College at the university. He was therefore able to reach some of the upper-class English. But he addressed himself largely to the common people, sending out lay evangelists to instruct them.

After 1375 Wycliffe's reforming views developed rapidly. Pope Gregory XI condemned him in 1377 for his efforts, but he was protected by some of the nobles and the powerful John of Gaunt, who was duke of Lancaster and son of Edward III. These were the days of the Hundred Years War, and it was unthinkable that Englishmen would surrender one of their most outstanding countrymen to a pope at Avignon, who was considered to be under the domination of England's French foes. The power of Wycliffe was at least threefold: his intense patriotism, his deep piety, and the belief of many that he had no scholarly equal in England.

To Wycliffe, Scripture, which he interpreted literally, was the sole authority for the believer. Decrees of the pope were not infallible except as based on Scripture. The clergy were not to rule, but to serve and help people. Eventually he reached the conclusion that Christ and not the pope was the head of the church; in fact, the pope, if he were too eager for worldly power, might even be regarded as the Antichrist. He also attacked transubstantiation (the view that the bread and wine in the Eucharist become the body and blood of Christ) and seems to have come to a position similar to Luther's. Moreover, he condemned the dogma of purgatory and the use of relics, pilgrimages, and indulgences. He seems to have been deeply influenced by St. Augustine. It is not clear how evangelical Wycliffe was personally, but under the influence of biblical teaching his followers increasingly moved in that direction.

The followers of Wycliffe were suppressed by force in 1401. Thereafter those who held his views went underground and no doubt helped to prepare the way for the Lutheran and Calvinistic teachings that invaded Britain about a century later. Bohemians studying at Oxford in Wycliffe's day carried his ideas to their homeland, where they influenced the teachings of John Hus.

John Hus. John Hus (1372?-1415), professor of philosophy at the University of Prague and preacher at Bethlehem Chapel, did not slavishly depend on Wycliffe, however. The old view that he was influenced by Wycliffe to the point that he simply adopted the views of the Englishman as his own must now be abandoned. A Czech reform movement, dating to about the middle of the fourteenth century, paralleled Wycliffe's efforts. Hus was in the tradition of the native movement and a product of it. But during the early fifteenth century indigenous and imported varieties of reform joined to form a single development.

At any rate, Hus's approach was similar to that of Wycliffe, and his influence on the Continent was greater than that of the Englishman. It should be remembered that Luther was greatly impressed with the reformer from Prague. Hus's great work was entitled *On the Church*. In it he stated that all the elect are members of Christ's church, of which Christ rather than the pope is head. He argued against simony, indulgences, and abuses of the mass. He demanded a reform in the lives of clergy, and he asserted the right of laity to take both the bread and wine in the Communion.

Hus became the leader of a reform movement that spread across Bohemia. Almost the whole nation supported him in his reform program, in spite of the fact that he was excommunicated by the pope. After Hus's death this reform agitation did not cease, and about the middle of the fifteenth century the Bohemian Brethren rose out of the embers of the fire Hus had lit. They still exist as the Moravian Brethren.

When the pope summoned Hus to the Council of Constance to stand examination on his views, the Emperor Sigismund ordered him to go and promised safe conduct to and from the council. But when the council condemned him as a heretic and burned him at the stake, Sigismund did not interfere. Like Luther, Hus came to blows with the pope over the issue of indulgences (among other things); but Europe was not so ready for the Reformation in 1415 at it would be a century later.

Savonarola. Girolamo Savonarola (1452-1498) was a forceful preacher against the worldliness and corruption of church and society in Florence. A Dominican, he was transferred to the priory of San Marco in Florence in 1482 and gradually rose in influence and power in the city. His studies in the Old Testament prophets and the book of Revelation helped to make him a powerful preacher against the evils and corruption of society.

Savonarola became the spiritual leader of the democratic party that came to power in Florence with the invasion of Charles VIII of France and the flight of the Medici in 1494. Exercising virtual dictatorship over the city, he tried to reform both the state and church there. The new constitution of 1495 was similar to that of the Republic of Venice.

With the passage of time opposition to Savonarola heightened and his power began to slip. His opposition and ultimate downfall resulted as much from his political and social involvements in the city as from his religious tangle with the Roman church. Pope Alexander VI excommunicated him in 1497, and in April of 1498 he was arrested and tried for sedition and heresy and cruelly tortured. Finally on May 23 he was hanged and his body burned.

Although Savonarola demanded reform in the church, he never took the more advanced position of Wycliffe and Hus. He had no quarrel with the teachings or the organization of the church, but personally seems to have believed in justification by faith. He was characterized by religious zeal and personal piety. Because he openly condemned the evil character and misrule of Pope Alexander VI and the corruption of the papal court, he won the undying opposition of the papacy and suffered execution.

Brethren of the Common Life. Contemporary with Wycliffe and Hus was a mystical movement that flowered in Holland, northern France, and northern Germany during the latter fourteenth and the fifteenth centuries. Emphasizing Bible reading, meditation, prayer, personal piety, and religious education it produced such outstanding figures as Jan Van Ruysbroeck (d. 1381), who wrote *The Seven Steps of Spiritual Love,* and Gerhard Grote (d. 1384), who was instrumental in founding the Brethren of the Common Life. The principal aim of the Brethren, a quasi-monastic group, was to secure a revival of practical religion, and its members were deeply devoted to the cause of education. They established in the Netherlands and Germany several schools that were outstanding for scholarship and piety. Four of their best-known students were Nicholas of Cusa, Erasmus, Luther, and Thomas à Kempis, who wrote or edited the widely distributed *Imitation of Christ.*

Many other religious movements, for which there is no space here, spread across Europe during the fifteenth century, demonstrating how widespread was the demand for church reform there. In fact the Continent was a seething kettle by 1500—ready to boil over. In the realms of economics, society, politics, intellect, and religion, the time had come for an eruption. All that was needed was someone who could mold these explosive elements into a single movement. Such a movement would blitz Europe. It was Martin Luther who provided a channel for all this explosive energy in what is now called the Protestant Reformation. For a clearer understanding of Luther's place in the history of Europe, it is necessary to survey the various facets of life on the Continent on the eve of the Reformation.

Europe on the Eve of the Reformation

In giving reasons for the decline of the papacy during the later Middle Ages we have noted some of the properties on the stage of Europe while the drama of the Reformation was enacted. Much more needs to be said on the subject.

POLITICS

The political map of Europe was a crazy quilt composed of hundreds of principalities, evidencing extreme decentralization. But around the fringes, in Portugal, Spain, France, and England, national states were rising, challenging the supranational power of the papacy. In central Europe the Holy Roman Empire (now essentially a German entity) had an emperor checkmated by numerous states with slight allegiance to him. Not only was the emperor hampered by these semi-independent vassals, but Muslim hosts knocked at the doors of the empire soon after Luther nailed his theses on the church door at Wittenberg. After toppling Constantinople and the Byzantine Empire in 1453,[1] the Muslims (Ottoman Turks) advanced across Eastern Europe until they stood before the gates of Vienna in 1529 and again reached the vicinity of the city in 1532.

What had really happened was this. Charles, a Hapsburg and king of the Netherlands and Spain, was elected in 1519 as Charles V of the Holy Roman Empire. Francis I of France, almost surrounded by the holdings of Charles and defeated by him in 1525, made an alliance with the Ottoman Empire in 1526 to apply a pincers movement against his enemy. Charles needed the help of all his German vassals to defeat the Turks. As some of the German princes became Lutheran, he was not able to put religous pressure on them, because then they would not give political and military support. Thus Charles was not able to force Frederick of Saxony (one of his most powerful vassals) to surrender Luther when the pope demanded the Reformer.

Meanwhile Europe was expanding. A few years after Luther's birth Columbus discovered the New World and launched the Spanish Empire in the West; shortly after Luther posted his theses, Magellan's expedition sailed around the world. At the same time, the Portuguese were establishing outposts of empire in Brazil, Africa, and the Far East.

INTELLECT

A new world of thought was discovered long before 1492. The full tide of the Renaissance had rolled in. Rediscovering the literature and thought patterns of the classical age, it contributed to a greater secularization of life. Humanism was one of the main

1. When Constantinople fell to the Muslim Turks, the center of power of the old Eastern Orthodox church was destroyed. Thereafter, the Orthodox church broke up into national churches: Russian Orthodox, Hellenic Orthodox, Serbian Orthodox, Syrian Orthodox, etc. These national churches do not differ appreciably in theology and liturgy.

features of the Renaissance, involving a new emphasis on man and his culture and an effort to make the world a better place in which man might live. The pull of the future life was not so great for the true child of the Renaissance as it had been for his forbears during the Middle Ages. He would rather eat his pie now than have it in the sky by and by.

In harking back to the literature of the classical age, the humanists put new emphasis on the study of Greek (and some of them, Hebrew) in an effort to read the classics in the original languages. The greatest of all ancient documents was the Bible, and the renewed emphasis on ancient languages led many to the Scripture. The humanism of northern Europe seemed to put more stress on the form and analysis of classical literature, the humanism of southern Europe seemed to stress the philosophy embedded in that literature. The literary humanists included a good deal of biblical study in their academic diet, and it was in the north that the Reformation gained most headway—Zwingli, Calvin, Melanchthon, and Erasmus are examples of the more biblical of the literary humanists. That Erasmus, among others, was a great satirist of the evils of the institutional church, as well as of the evils of society in general, underscores the fact that criticism of Romanism by Renaissance leaders contributed to the success of the Reformation. Also advancing the effectiveness of the Reformation was the Renaissance spirit of individualism, which paved the way for Luther's emphasis on the priesthood of the believer and its attendant ideas of the right of the believer to go directly to God and to interpret the Scriptures for himself.

Another important facet of the intellectual development of Europe on the eve of the Reformation was the invention of movable type and the spread of printing.[2] Without it the Reformers could not have had the same effect. In fact, the tremendous literary activity of the Reformers was largely responsible for building the printing trade in many areas.

Last, an important phenomenon of the period was the rapid

2. Whether Coaster or Gutenberg invented printing with movable type cannot be demonstrated with certainty, but the date was around 1430-1440. The process was quite well developed during the latter part of the fifteenth century.

growth of universities, which provided education for a larger number of people, fostered the critical spirit, and provided a means whereby the leaders of the new generation could be reached with Reformation principles and wherein they could be trained to promulgate them.

RELIGION

The religion of Europe was in a condition of decay. The evils of the church were many—simony, economic oppression, the purchase of salvation through indulgence traffic, immorality of many of the clergy, and so on. The effects of the Babylonian Captivity and Papal Schism had been great, as noted earlier. The wave of secularism that engulfed Europe during the fifteenth century affected all levels of church life: the parishioners, lower and higher clergy, monks, and even the successors of St. Peter.

The decadence of the church led to numerous calls from within for its reform. Symptomatic of this concern were such movements as the Observant Franciscans in England, the Oratory of Divine Love in Italy, and the Brethren of the Common Life in the Lowlands. Books of devotion found wide audience. Mendicant friars preached an emotional religion. Evidence of the religious concern of the common man is considerable; a religious ferment emphasized the emotions and provided a basis for popular support of the Reformation.

SOCIETY AND ECONOMICS

European society and economics were in flux. Feudalism was on the decline, and it was paralleled by the rise of towns and nation-states. In these new towns and states a new middle class emerged, as did a degree of social mobility not known for more than a millennium. Compared with the old nobility, these striving, successful people were social, political, and economic outsiders; naturally they wanted to become social, political, and economic insiders. Traditionally, what really mattered in society were the titled nobility with their great holdings in landed estates. Members of the rising middle class, with their wealth in financial and commercial interests, felt they were the equals of the old aristocracy and sought social recognition and political power. Peasants were generally restless, looking for a way out of their economic and social oppression. Both national governments and the middle class needed a ready supply of cash. Kings and nobles had to support armies and navies, finance public improvements, and promote the general welfare of their people. Businessmen needed to have capital reserve for new economic ventures. All this naturally hindered the flow of wealth to the church, and efforts of the church to drain money from an area were met with something less than enthusaism by king and middle class alike.

The Reformation in Germany

To such an age as this, one seething with unrest and vexed with a host of problems and longings, came Martin Luther. He was a voice speaking for a multitude who had been voiceless. In fact, as he began his reformation activities, many hoped he would become their spokesman in political, economic, and social, as well as religious, matters.

Born the son of a miner in 1483 Martin Luther lived in a day when men were able to better their fortunes. Hans Luther gradually amassed a fairly adequate estate and was able to provide Martin with an excellent education. After early studies at Mansfeld, Magdeburg (where he was taught by Brethren of the Common Life), and Eisenach, Martin matriculated at the University of Erfurt, where he earned his B.A. and M.A. degrees. He was second in a class of seventeen when he took the M.A. in 1505. Thereafter, on his father's urging, he entered the law school of the university.

But in July of that year, when thrown to the ground by a flash of lightning during a very bad storm, he vowed to enter a monastery if spared from death. But this was not the only reason for his decision. Apparently, Luther hoped he would find at the Augustinian monastery at Erfurt the peace for his soul that he could not find on the outside. As Luther pursued the monastic life, he saw Christ as a stern judge, and he spent days in fasts and bodily mortification, seeking release for his sinful soul. During his struggle he came under the influence of Johann Von Staupitz, vicar-general of his order, who urged him to think on God's love for the sinner as evidenced in Christ's death. Luther assiduously studied "the Bible with the red binding" that he was given on entering the monastery.

Meanwhile, Staupitz had become dean of the faculty of theology at the newly founded University of Wittenberg, and he arranged for Luther to join the faculty of the university in 1508. Two years later Luther went to Rome on a business trip for the Augustinian order and had a chance to view the papacy firsthand; for him it was a disillusioning experience. When in 1512 he received his doctor of theology degree, he succeeded Staupitz[3] as professor of theology, which position he held until his death in 1546.

During 1513-1518, Luther lectured on Psalms, Romans, Galatians, Hebrews, and Titus and sometime during that period came to an acceptance of the doctrine of justification by faith.[4] He was a Saul turned Paul. He abandoned the prevailing Scholastic and allegorical interpretation of Scripture for a more strictly literal and grammatical interpretation. To his pedagogical method his students responded enthusiastically. Luther's influence expanded as he was given charge over eleven monasteries in 1515. In the same year the town council of Wittenberg called him to the pulpit of the City Church, where he continued to minister the rest of his life. From that vantage point, he could carry his views directly to the laity.

The issue that brought Luther to the attention of all Europe was indulgences. Initially, an indulgence provided for the remission of punishment imposed by the Roman Catholic church on someone who had broken some religious commandment. In earlier days one might gain such an indulgence for risking his life in fighting the infidel during the Crusades. Gradually however, fi-

3. An evangelical, Staupitz almost became a Reformer but died as a faithful son of the Roman church in 1524. If he had lived longer, he might have made the break later, when Saxony became more strongly Lutheran.
4. Scholars have been unable to date this event precisely. Perhaps it came during 1515 when he was lecturing on the early chapters of Romans.

nancial sacrifice was accepted in lieu of physical risk. And the financing of the building of churches, monasteries, hospitals, and the like could be designated by the pope as warranting indulgences. During the later Middle Ages indulgences came to involve not only remission of punishment imposed by the Roman church, but also absolution of all guilt incurred before God.

Pope Leo X (1513-1521), like his predecessor Julius II, sought to raise funds for the building of St. Peter's in Rome by indulgence sales. His needs coincided with those of Albert of Hohenzollern, then only twenty-three, who had gone heavily into debt to buy from the papacy the archbishoprics of Mainz and Magdeburg and the bishopric of Halberstadt. So it was decided that indulgences would be offered for sale in Albert's domains and the proceeds split equally between the archbishop and the pope. Luther did not know about the pope's involvement in this financial arrangement. What bothered him was the promise of full remission of sin and punishment in purgatory for living persons and what was worse, the assurance to purchasers that their dead loved ones in purgatory could be forgiven their sins without confession or contrition.

Frederic of Saxony forbade the sale of indulgences in his domain; so there was none of the traffic at Wittenberg. But Wittenberg citizens traveled to other towns to buy indulgences. When Luther observed the effect of this sale on the moral and ethical standards of his parishoners, he decided to post his famous Ninety-five Theses (or topics for debate) on the church door at Wittenberg on October 31, 1517, in protest against the indulgence sale.[5] Printed copies quickly flooded Europe, and popular enthusiasm was engendered everywhere. A conservative, faithful son of the church, Luther believed the authority of the pope and the validity of the sacrament of penance were at stake in the way the indulgences had been sold. He sent a copy of the theses and a letter of explanation to Albert. Early in 1518, still not believing that the abuse in the indulgence sale had been approved by the pope, Luther sent an explanation (the *Resolutions*) to Leo X. In trying

5. Evidently Luther intended that the theses should be debated by the theological community at Wittenberg; they were posted in Latin, not German.

to squelch Luther, Leo preferred to put pressure on him through local agencies (e.g., the Augustinian order), but members of the higher echelon of papal power in Rome persuaded the pope to demand Luther's appearance in Rome as a suspect of heresy.

Luther then apppealed to Frederick the Wise of Saxony for advice in handling the complicated proceedings and requested that the hearing be held in Germany. Nationalistically minded Frederick arranged a meeting at Augsburg in 1518; this ended in a standoff between the two parties. In subsequent years polarization of the two camps increased. Luther gradually turned his back on the authority of the pope and councils and planted himself squarely on the teachings of Scripture. The pope became increasingly determined to get his hands on Luther; but he could not, because Frederick protected him. The new emperor, Charles V, was loath to come to Leo's aid and thus alienate Frederick, because Saxony was the most powerful state in Germany at the time and the emperor needed all the support he could get for his war against the Turks. Finally, in 1521 Luther went to the Diet of Worms (a parliament of the empire) under an imperial safe conduct. It was at Worms that he uttered the famous words: "I cannot and will not recant anything, for it is neither safe nor honest to act against one's conscience. God help me. Amen." On the way back Frederick's men kidnapped Luther to protect him, and put him in Wartburg Castle, where he translated the New Testament into idiomatic German in the unbelievably short time of eleven weeks.[6] While there, he was informed of extremism and violence at Wittenberg; so he returned to quell the disturbance.

With Luther excommunicated by the Roman church and living under an imperial ban that deprived him of physical protection, what began as a reformation became in effect a revolution. Luther, with Frederick's protection, launched a new religious movement. During these years the pope was still trying to stop Luther.

6. Luther used Erasmus's Greek Testament of 1516, the first printed Greek Testament, for his New Testament translation work. Later he translated the Old Testament. Luther's German Bible, because of its widespread use, was very significant in standardizing the German language, which at that time was spoken and written in many local dialects. Luther became to German what Dante was to Italian and what, to a degree, Wycliffe and Calvin were to English and French respectively.

At the Diet of Speyer (1529) it was resolved to forbid further spread of the Lutheran movement. Against this action a *protest* was entered by a number of German princes and free cities. Subscribers came to be known as protestants, and soon the name *Protestant* passed on to the whole movement. In the following year the Protestant princes got together in what was called the Schmalkald League. Already hard pressed by the Ottoman Turks, who had appeared before the gates of Vienna in 1529, the emperor Charles V finally granted religious freedom to the princes in 1532 and interfered with Lutheranism no more for several years.

Meanwhile the Roman Catholics became alarmed by the spread of Protestantism and banded together to form the Holy League. War broke out in 1546, the year Luther died. After initial victories by the Roman Catholics, the Protestants finally defeated the imperial forces. The Diet of Augsburg (1555) ended the struggle and provided for a recognition of Roman Catholicsm and Lutheranism as legal religions in the Holy Roman Empire.

Luther's right hand man at Wittenberg was Philipp Melanchthon, (1497-1560), who directed the organizational, educational, and publishing side of the Reformation. He is often called the teacher of Germany. He aided in establishing primary and secondary schools, and did all he could to train the clergy. Recognizing the need for organizing the church that Luther had brought into being, he prepared a manual for that purpose. He also wrote a systematic theology, commentaries on New Testament books, and was largely responsible for preparing the various statements of faith that the Lutherans presented at some of the diets where they met papal foes.

Luther was a popular and dynamic leader in an age that was looking for such leadership. He was an indefatigable critic of Roman Catholicism in an age that became increasingly critical of Roman Catholicism. He played on the national interests of the Germans in such pamphlets as his "Address to the Christian Nobles of the German Nation" in an age when nationalism was gathering momentum rapidly. He offered a message of hope and faith to a people lost in the darkness of sin and looking for light. For all these reasons, Luther was successful.

But often he has been criticized because he did not go far

enough in his reforms (he retained the crucifix, candles, and other elements of Roman Catholicism), because he placed the church under the control of civil authority, and because he failed to cooperate with the Swiss Reformers and thus present a solid block of Protestants against Roman Catholic power in Europe.

In his preaching Luther set forth three great distinctives: *sola fide* (justification by faith alone); *sola gratia* (salvation by grace alone); and *sola scriptura* (the Bible alone as the source of the believer's authority for doctrine and practice). He also had much to say about the priesthood of the believer. Every believer was a priest and had the right to go to God directly; Christ was the only mediator between God and humanity. Moreover, every believer had the right to interpret the Scripture for himself under the guidance of the Holy Spirit. God spoke directly to the believer-priest through His Word; believers could address God directly in prayer and especially in their songs. He gave the German people not only a Bible in their own tongue, but also a hymnbook. In his hands the hymn became a great spiritual weapon, and he became the father of evangelical hymnody.

The Reformation in Scandinavia

Although Lutheranism spread early to many countries of Europe and later to the New World, it became the dominant faith of Scandinavia. When Luther posted his theses at Wittenberg, Sweden and Norway were united to Denmark (as they had been ever since the Union of Kalmar in 1397). But in 1517 a Swedish revolt was trying to throw off Danish control. This nationalistic effort was opposed by the Roman church, and the archbishop of Upsala won the title of Swedish Judas Iscariot. Ultimately, Gustavus Vasa was successful in winning Swedish independence and, because of national antipathy to Roman Catholicism and because of his personal preferences, he had little difficulty in setting up a national Lutheran church in the 1520s. Because Finland was a possession of the Swedish crown, Lutheranism was soon established there too.

The advance of Lutheranism in Denmark (and Norway, which was linked to it) is much more complicated and would require considerable space to describe. Suffice it to say that Frederick I (1523-1533) set up a national church with definite Lutheran leanings. After a period of civil war Christian III came to the throne (1536-1559) and at once reorganized the Danish church and made it distinctively Lutheran. Roman Catholic and Anabaptist dissenters were suppressed. In Iceland, which belonged to Norway, the policy was to force Lutheranism on a reluctant populace. After a midcentury revolt against Norwegian authority was put down, Lutheranism was established there by royal decree in 1554.

At the eastern end of the Baltic, in Estonia, Latvia, and Lithuania, Lutheranism spread rapidly after 1539. And in 1561, Sweden annexed Estonia, which fact strengthened Lutheranism there. About 1525, the grand master of the Teutonic Knights established Lutheranism throughout East Prussia.

The Reformation in Switzerland

ZWINGLI

Huldreich Zwingli (1484-1531) sparked the Reformation in German-speaking Switzerland. After study at Bern, Vienna, and Basel, he was ordained and became parish priest at Glarus, where he remained for ten years. At Glarus he studied extensively the classics in the original languages, thus laying the foundation for his future Reformation work. During those years he also served as chaplain to Swiss mercenaries in Italy and began a campaign against Swiss mercenary service. This effort brought him many enemies in some of the poorer areas of the country, where that means of employment was thought to be necessary. Such animosity would be important in the later factionalizing of the country.

In 1516 he moved to the monastery church of Einsiedeln for a three-year ministry. There he studied the Greek New Testament published by Erasmus. He later claimed that at Einsiedeln in 1516 he had begun to found his preaching on the gospel. Thus his reformation work began about the same time as Luther's. Because the monastery church had a well-known image of the virgin Mary, it had become a pilgrimage center. To such comers Zwingli began to preach against the belief that religious pilgrimages were a means of obtaining pardon.

After becoming priest in a large cathedral in Zurich (1519) Zwingli gradually became more open about his views. He broke with the pope and married, and preached openly against celibacy. Popular feeling was roused to such a point that the city council felt that it was necessary to appoint a public meeting for the discussion of religious subjects. When it convened, Zwingli presented his Sixty-seven Articles and was so convincing that the council charged him to continue in evangelical methods and urged other preachers to follow his example. Tremendous changes followed; many priests married and set aside the mass. Some thought the evangelical movement had gone too far, but the city council stood behind the Reformation and eventually abolished the mass and image worship altogether.

Switzerland was a network of thirteen small states, or cantons, loosely federated and generally democratic. Culturally the northern and eastern regions were German in language and orientation, the western part French, and the southern part Italian. Geographically the country was divided between mountain or forest and valley cantons. Gradually the Reformation spread from Zurich, the chief city of the chief canton, to other cities of German Switzerland until the valley cantons were won. But that did not mean they were willing to join with Zurich in a united front. Some did not want to risk domination by Zurich. Several forest or mountain cantons remained militantly Roman Catholic and, being poor farming areas, found Zwingli's antimercenary patriotism to be a threat to their economic life.

As political tensions heightened, some Protestant cantons formed a Christian Civic League; the Roman Catholic cantons organized also and allied themselves with Ferdinand of Austria. War broke out in 1529 and ended early in 1531 with the Protestants defeated and Zwingli slain. He had served his townsmen as chaplain at the front. Thereafter the Reformation program in German Switzerland lost ground, but Heinrich Bullinger became Zwingli's able successor in Zurich. The military struggle had assured the virtual independence of the several cantons and therefore made it possible for the western canton of Geneva to go its separate way in following the lead of John Calvin a few years later.

As has been indicated, Zwingli directed the Reformation in Switzerland along civic lines, with a view to establishing a model Christian community. He persuaded the city council to legislate the various details of the Reformation and supervise the carrying out of its decisions. In other words, he aimed at political as well as spiritual regeneration.

Zwingli's theology put great emphasis on the sovereignty of God and His election unto salvation. He held that the Lord's Supper contributed nothing to the elect; it was merely a symbol or rememberance of the sacrifice of Christ. He could not agree with Luther, who held that the body and blood of Christ are really present in the Communion. This was the rock on which the negotiations of the German and Swiss Reformers broke at Marburg in 1529. During his last years Zwingli moved away from his earlier position toward a doctrine of the spiritual presence of Christ in the Supper. The same may be said of Melanchthon. The Zwinglian movement merged into Calvinism later in the sixteenth century.

THE ANABAPTISTS

By no means did all those who broke with Rome agree with Zwingli, or with Luther or Calvin, for that matter. As early as 1523, in Zurich, Protestant separatists Conrad Grebel and Felix Manz questioned a number of the teachings and practices of Romanism and began to insist on adult baptism. Their activities caused the city council to persecute them, and many of their followers and fellow preachers were exiled, spreading the movement into Germany and Moravia. In time Anabaptist became a general term applied by Zwinglians, Lutherans, Roman Catholics, and others to those who would not fellowship with any of these communions, who rejected a connection between church and state, and who rejected infant baptism or for some reason insisted on rebaptism later in life.

The term *Anabaptist* was a general descriptive, and widely diverse views were held among them. Some were pantheistic, some extremely mystical, some anti-Trinitarian, some extremely millenarian, and some quite biblical. Modern Baptists who like to place themselves in the Anabaptist tradition need to remember that some groups of Anabaptists were not truly biblical. Futhermore, many of them, although they insisted on water baptism after a conversion experience, did not baptize by immersion. Moreover, the doctrinal position of biblical Anabaptists is more closely related to the modern Mennonite viewpoint than to Baptist theology (see below).

Today there is a tendency to describe the Anabaptists as the left wing of the Reformation, or better, the radical Reformation, and to find at least three major groups among them: Anabaptists proper, spiritualists, and religious rationalists. Generally, all of them opposed meddling with the religious affairs of the citizenry by the state or state churches, though a few tried to set up a revolutionary theocracy or accepted protection of the state.

Rationalists sought to put intuitive and speculative reason alongside Scripture as a basis of religious authority or a source of religious information. From this seedbed came the anti-Trinitarian efforts of Socinus and Servetus, as well as various pantheistic or transcendental approaches that involved a spiritual contemplation of the order of nature or allegorized the Bible into a cosmic philosophy. Spiritualists put much emphasis on the future. They either sought revolutionary change in society as they set up communities designed to be utopias of sorts, or quiescently awaited the end of the age or the dawn of a millennial day. The true Anabaptists were quite ascetic, tended to communal holding of goods, were pacifistic, opposed the use of oaths and capital punishment, favored the free will of man as opposed to predestination, stressed individual faith and witness, insisted on water baptism after a conversion experience, and taught separation of church and state. Primarily they were the spiritual antecedents of modern Mennonites rather than modern Baptists. As may be suspected, by no means can all groups of radical Reformers be neatly categorized under one of the three headings suggested here.[7]

CALVIN

John Calvin (1509-1564) was the great second generation Reformer. As such, he could benefit from the work of such leaders as Luther, Zwingli, and Bucer. He began in the Roman church and gained a couple of benefices early in life because his father was in the service of the bishop of Noyon, but he was never ordained to the priesthood. His father wanted him to study law, and he completed the degree in that discipline, but he also took university training in literature. His intellectual pursuits took him to the universities at Paris, Orléans, and Bourges. At the latter he came under the influence of Wolmar, with whom he studied Greek and Hebrew and the New Testament in the original language. His conversion probably dated sometime during 1532 or 1533. Calvin says it was sudden, through private study, and because he failed to find peace in absolutions, penances, and intercessions of the Roman Catholic church. Soon thereafter he and some of his friends were caught up in an anti-Protestant drive and forced to leave Paris.

For three years he wandered about as a refugee in France, Germany, and Switzerland. During this period in his life, Calvin met Martin Bucer, the great Reformer of Strasbourg, who was professor of theology at the university there. And at Basel in 1536, at the age of only twenty-six, Calvin published the first edition of his *Institutes of the Christian Religion;* the last edition (1559) was several times the size of the original. Later in 1536, Calvin decided that after paying a last visit to his native France he would settle in Strasbourg.

But he passed through Geneva on the way, and there William

7. Especially useful books on the Anabaptists include George H. Williams and A. M. Mergal, eds., *Spiritual and Anabaptist Writers* (Philadelphia: Westminster, 1957); George H. Williams, *The Radical Reformation* (Philadelphia: Westminster, 1962); Cornelius Krahn, *Dutch Anabaptism* (The Hague: Martinus Nijhoff, 1968); A. L. E. Verheyden, *Anabaptism in Flanders 1530-1650* (Scottdale, Pa.: Herald Press, 1961), and J. K. Zeman, *The Anabaptists and the Czech Brethren in Moravia 1526-1628* (The Hague: Mouton, 1969).

Farel persuaded Calvin to remain and help him with the Reformation there. In 1535 Geneva officially had become Protestant. The city council had made laws against drunkenness, gambling, dancing, and the like; but the laws had little effect.[8] So when Calvin came he prepared a catechism and articles of faith and insisted on the right of the church to exercise discipline over unworthy communicants. Farel and Calvin worked very hard from 1536 to 1538 to establish the community on a theocratic basis. But the profligate population was not ready for rigid discipline; so the Reformers were banished—Farel going to Neuchatel and Calvin to Strasbourg.

The interval at Strasbourg seems to have been a happy one for Calvin. He pastored a congregation of French refugees, wrote his commentary on Romans, met with Reformers in Germany, and married a widow. But a son born to them lived only a few days. Meanwhile back in Geneva the church was in confusion, and the Roman church had put on a campaign to bring the city back into its fold. This threat, together with the rise of his friends to power in the city government, led Calvin to return reluctantly in 1541.

For the rest of his life Calvin worked tirelessly in his adopted city. Though he held no government office and did not even gain citizenship in Geneva until 1559, Calvin dominated the city. He exercised strict discipline over the morals of the community and drew up a new form of government and liturgy for the church. Moreover, he was largely responsible for a system of universal education for the young and programs to care for the poor and aged. And he established the Academy, later to be the University of Geneva.

The major event that marred the administration of Calvin at Geneva was the Servetus incident. Michael Servetus was a Spaniard under sentence of death by the Inquisition for his unitarian views. He escaped from prison and presumably stopped in Geneva to stir up trouble. There he was put on trial and ultimately judged guilty of subversion of religion and the general welfare. Genevan authorities consulted with other Swiss leaders, who

8. Thus it can be seen that Calvin was not responsible for the stringent code of conduct imposed upon citizens of Geneva during his ministry there; it antedated him. Therefore, he should not be blamed for it.

supported the accusations against Servetus and recommended the death penalty. Finally, on October 25, 1563, he was judged guilty on fourteen counts and condemned to death by fire, contrary to provisions of the city ordinances, which limited punishment to banishment. Although this act is to be lamented, it is to be remembered that the age was an intolerant one. Roman Catholics executed thousands of Protestants throughout the century, and they probably would have burned Servetus at the stake if he had not escaped from them. Calvin took part only in this one execution; but he never appeared in person during the proceedings, and he argued for a more humane form of execution. Moreover, the event had political overtones. Calvin's enemies sought to use Servetus to overthrow Calvin and expel his friends from power in the city government. In spite of all that, Calvin's reputation has been forever tarnished by the event.

John Calvin was probably the most influential leader of the Reformation era. He put much stress on education. His catechetical system for the young has been carried all over the world. And at the school in Geneva men were trained who spread Presbyterianism all over Western Europe. In part his influence rose from the fact that Geneva generously welcomed refugees from almost every country in Europe. Often they returned home to spread the variety of Christianity they had come to know in Geneva. It was Calvin's theology and form of church government that triumphed in the Protestant church of France, the Reformed Church of Germany, the Church of Scotland, the Reformed Church in Hungary, the Reformed Church in Holland, and in Puritanism in England and New England.[9]

Calvin's biblical and theological writings also have been very influential. He wrote commentaries on twenty-three Old Testament books and twenty-six New Testament books. His *Institutes of the Christian Religion* became the dominant systematic theology of the Reformation in all except Lutheran lands. And he wrote numerous pamphlets on current issues. His literary output was so prodigious that he influenced the development of modern French; he has been credited along with Rabelais as being co-

9. Puritanism in America adopted the Congregational form of church government, but retained Calvinistic theology.

founder of modern French prose. And Calvin is often called the father of the historical-grammatical method of biblical study—a method that attempts to discover what the Scripture meant to those who wrote it, and what it means according to the common definition of its words. Contemporary evangelical students have so taken this method for granted that they have little realization of the part that Calvin had in its development and of the fact that it was virtually nonexistent in the church before the Reformation.

The Reformation in France

As the sixteenth century wore on, the Roman Catholic church in France fell into an increasingly deplorable condition. In addition to the general slackness it experienced during the Renaissance era, the Roman church suffered increasingly from the effects of the Concordat of Bologna (1516). This agreement between Francis I of France and Pope Leo III gave the French monarch the right to appoint the 10 archbishops, 38 bishops, and 527 heads of religious houses in the realm. Henceforth the church became part of a vast patronage system, and individuals won positions in the church not for ability or religious zeal but for service to the crown or by purchase. Conditions became indescribably bad. For instance, it is asserted that standards for parish priests declined to the point that only some ten percent could read. Whether or not this percentage is correct, it seems safe to say that only a minority were literate. The king had in fact become the head of the church, and his great dependence on its patronage system and revenues helps to explain why Francis I and Henry II were so zealous in their persecution of Protestants. They could not afford to permit the system to crumble. They certainly were not zealous for the Roman Catholic faith.

Impetus for the French Protestant movement came from Geneva, and its advance was achieved especially through the printed page—the French Bible, Calvin's *Institutes,* and numerous other publications. Naturally the most literate element of the population was more largely won. Converts were especially numerous at the universities and among lawyers and other professionals, the merchant classes and the artisans, the lower clergy and the friars, and the lesser nobility. The illiterate peasantry was hardlly touched. In addition to the positive attraction of the gospel, special forces worked to propel many into the Protestant camp. Lawyers and other professionals were traditionally anticlerical, merchants and financiers were discontented because of the financial strain of Francis's Italian wars, and many of the lesser nobles were in revolt against a social and political system of which they were victims.

In spite of persecution the Protestant movement expanded rapidly. Under Henry II (1547-1559) Protestants may have numbered four hundred thousand. By the end of his reign they came to be known commonly as Huguenots (meaning uncertain), and the total number of their congregations is said to have been 2,150 in 1561. The Presbyterian system of church government gave a firm organization and discipline to the Huguenot movement.

In order to understand the course of events that the French Reformation took and to see why it became embroiled in the civil wars, it is necessary to look at political and social conditions of the times. First, that many of the younger nobility joined Protestant ranks is of very great significance. Entitled and accustomed to carry swords, they became protectors of Huguenot congregations during the turbulent years of mid century and later. Often they protected church meetings against hostile bands of Roman Catholics. Naturally, their concerns became mixed up in the affairs of the church, and their quarrel with the crown very much affected the actions of the church.

Second, it is important to note that there were three major groups of mutually jealous nobility in the realm. The Bourbons, heirs to the throne if the ruling house of Valois should die out, controlled most of western France. Their leadership was largely Huguenot. The powerful Guises, staunch Roman Catholics, had extensive holdings in the east. The Montmorencys controlled much of the central part of the country; their leadership was divided between Protestants and Roman Catholics.

Third, when Henry II died, he left behind him young sons who were dominated by his queen, Catherine de Medici. She was determined to maintain her personal control and advance the power of her sons and the central government. She was opposed by many of the nobility who were jealous of their old feudal rights and wanted to restrict the power of the monarchy.

Fourth, foreign affairs furnished another ingredient to the mix. As civil war boiled, both the English and Spanish sent aid to serve their respective national interests.

Fifth, as already intimated, the rising middle class, as political and social outsiders and put upon by heavy financial exactions, opposed the crown for reasons of their own. The fact that they were also largely Huguenot only complicated their antipathy to the establishment.

Such animosities provided the tinder to ignite armed conflict. In fact eight wars were fought between Roman Catholic and Protestant forces in France.[10] Leading the Protestants early in the conflict was Gaspard de Coligny. But he lost his life along with thousands of other Protestants in the massacre of St. Bartholomew's Day, August 24, 1572, at the instigation of Catherine de Medici. Thereafter Henry of Navarre, of the Bourbon family, led the Protestants. His military activities were successful, and ultimately, with the death of others in the royal line, he became heir to the throne of France. Because he did not have quite enough strength to complete his conquest, he turned Roman Catholic and won the crown. Judging from his conduct, Henry's religious principles sat rather lightly on his shoulders. His switch to Catholicism was obviously for political reasons, and perhaps the purpose was to turn off the blood bath that was drenching France.

At any rate, in 1598 Henry published the Edict of Nantes, a grant of toleration for the Huguenots. It guaranteed them the right to hold public office, freedom of worship in most areas of

10. Though "Roman Catholic versus Protestant" is a convenient way of describing the so-called religious wars of the last half of the sixteenth century, it is evidently not strictly accurate. Commonly the battle raged for political or social reasons. More than once a Protestant group and a Roman Catholic group joined hands against another Roman Catholic group. And Protestant Henry of Navarre (later Henry IV) rose to power in part through the efforts of Politiques, liberal Roman Catholics who served loyally in his army. It must be recognized that people have economic, social, political, and cultural interests as well as religious interests. Rarely does one set of concerns motivate to the exclusion of all others.

France, the privilege of educating their children in other than Roman Catholic schools, and free access to universities and hospitals. The edict was the first significant recognition of the rights of a religious minority in an otherwise intolerant age. Though the Huguenots enjoyed a period of great prosperity thereafter, they became a defensive minority, and finally Louis XIV revoked the edict in 1685. Thousands were driven into exile to the benefit of England, Holland, Prussia, and America.

The Reformation in England

The marital problems of Henry VIII especially led to England's break with Rome. Not only was he tired of Catherine of Aragon and enamored with Anne Boleyn, but he was concerned that Catherine had not provided him with a male heir. This could well have led to civil war after Henry's death. So he sought annulment of his marriage at the hands of the pope. But Clement VII, under the influence of the powerful Charles V of Spain (nephew of Catherine), would not agree. In the midst of the struggle Henry managed to install Thomas Cranmer as archbishop of Canterbury and to win from him annulment of his marriage to Catherine.

Though the rupture with Rome resulted from Henry's marital difficulties, the Reformation came to England for more complex reasons. Social, economic, political, cultural, and theological factors combined with personal matters to contribute to the success of the movement. The general spirit of anticlericalism, antipathy to Cardinal Thomas Wolsey, Tyndale's New Testament (1525), Erasmus's humanism, and the impact of numerous Lutheran converts were additional specific elements that helped to make the Reformation a success.

The break with Rome came in 1534, when Parliament passed the Supremacy Act, making Henry head of the Church of England. Soon thereafter Henry, in need of money and afraid of a fifth column in the realm, closed the monasteries of England. But Henry did not provide a Protestant theology for England; he merely changed the headship of the English church. His efforts were always directed toward political control rather than theo-

logical change. Evidently he sought the degree of political abso-
lutism, or at least control over the church, that was being
achieved by such contemporary sovereigns as Ferdinand of
Spain, Francis I of France, and Gustavus Vasa of Sweden. That he
sought no change in church doctrine is evident from his severe
persecution of individuals of a Lutheran persuasion. His one
innovation was the publication of the Great Bible (1537) and its
installation in the parish churches of the realm.

There was a marked change, however, during the reign of
Edward VI (1547-53). Coming to the throne at a very early age,
he was ruled by regents who were of Protestant persuasion. The
liturgy was changed, services conducted in English, a prayer
book composed, marriage allowed for the clergy, images done
away with, and the mass abolished. Archbishop Cranmer and
others composed the Forty-two Articles, which later became the
Thirty-nine Articles of the Church of England. A blend of Lutheran and Calvinist teachings, they were subscribed to by the king
but not by the Parliament.

Edward died in the midst of a Roman Catholic reaction. So
when Mary (1553-1558) took the throne as a Roman Catholic, she
was well received. In 1554 she married Philip of Spain and thereafter spent little time in England. Edward's religious policy had
been too sudden in one direction, and Mary's was too strong in
the other. In fact Mary brought the English church once more
within the Roman fold. Many Protestants fled the country; some
three hundred were martyred, including such outstanding leaders as Cranmer, Ridley, and Latimer. Of special importance to the
future of religion in England is the fact that many of the Marian
exiles went to Geneva. There they were converted to Calvinism
and later returned to England to help launch a Puritan opposition to Elizabeth's establishment.

After the persecutions during Mary's reign and the unpopular
Spanish alliance, the reign of Elizabeth I (1558-1603) was well
received by the English people. Persecution came to an end, as
did the Spanish alliance. The Church of England was reestab-
lished, a prayer book drawn up, and the Forty-two Articles revised to Thirty-nine and adopted by Parliament. Queen Elizabeth
loved an ornate service, and under her influence the Church of

England developed its liturgy in that direction.

In this development she was opposed by the Puritans. The Puritans, who are known to have existed as early as the days of Edward, stressed rigid morals, church discipline, and a conversion experience as a prerequisite to church membership; they de-emphasized ritualism. At first they did not oppose a church government controlled by bishops. But the oppressive measures of Elizabeth and the return of Marian exiles with their Calvinist views changed the character of English Puritans. Ultimately a great many of them argued for a presbyterian form of church government, insisted that only Christ could be considered Head of the church, and called for a general purification of the church and English society. Some of them came to prefer a congregational form of church government and were called Congregationalists, or Independents. Some Congregationalists (Brownists, or Separatists, later Pilgrims) held to complete separation of church and state. At about the end of Elizabeth's reign the Baptists appeared, drawing members from the ranks of the Puritans and Separatists. Baptists insisted on separation of church and state, the congregational form of church government, and a conversion experience prior to church membership and baptism. Normally, they also held that baptism should be by immersion.

James VI of Scotland became James I of England in 1603 and is significant to Christians for his interest in the Bible translation that bears his name (published in 1611). James is also important because he increased the opposition of the Puritans to the crown by arranging for Sunday sports and by encouraging Arminianism in England. This animosity grew until in the days of Charles I it erupted in civil war (1642-1646).[11] Prior to the outbreak of the war, many Englishmen had given up hope of any appreciable change in English religious life. Some, as Separatists (Pilgrims), had gone to Holland and/or Plymouth, Massachusetts, and others (Puritans) had established the Massachusetts Bay Colony. From 1640 to 1660, Parliament and Oliver Cromwell ruled the nation. The Puritan divines worked with the commissioners of the

11. The English civil war was not merely a religious squabble between Puritans and Anglicans, but a struggle between social, political, and economic groupings in which religion played a part.

Church of Scotland to compose the Westminster Confession, which was adopted by the Church of Scotland in 1647 and in part by the English Parliament in 1648.

The Reformation in Scotland

Probably in no country of Europe were the Roman Catholic clergy more depraved than in Scotland at the time of the Reformation. This fact, taken in conjunction with remaining influences of Wycliffe, the old Celtic church, and the infiltration of Lutheran and Calvinistic ideas, greatly contributed to the rise of the Reformation in Scotland.

The pioneer Reformer in Scotland was Patrick Hamilton, who had been influenced by Luther's views while a student in Paris and had returned to his homeland to preach. He was burned as a heretic in 1528. The second great leader of the Scottish Reformation was George Wishart, who had a Zwinglian and Calvinistic orientation. Wishart was martyred in 1546. Martyr's blood stirred many a heart in bonnie Scotland—and many a temper, too. By the time Cardinal Beaton presided over the martyrdom of Wishart, he had made so many enemies that a band of nobles (only one of whom was Protestant) entered his castle at St. Andrews and killed him.

Wishart's most ardent follower was John Knox—a leader with all the enthusiasm and popular power of Luther and the steadfastness of Calvin. After university training at St. Andrews, Knox, in great personal danger, fled for safety to the castle of St. Andrews, where the assassins of Beaton and others were holed up. A French fleet, coming to the assistance of the Scottish queen, took the castle, captured its occupants, and sold Knox as a galley slave. After nineteen months the English rescued him, and he ministered in England during the days of Edward VI. Leaving England when Mary Tudor (Bloody Mary) came to the throne, he ministered briefly among English exiles in Frankfurt and then became pastor of a group of English exiles in Geneva. His chapel was only a stone's throw from the cathedral where Calvin regularly preached. In 1555 he made a brief visit to England where he married, and subsequently preached in Scotland for nine months with great courage. Then he returned to Geneva for another three years.

Meanwhile the Reformation message spread widely in Scotland. Of prime importance to its success was the fact that in 1543 Parliament legalized the reading of the Bible in English or Scots. Moreover, a great amount of Protestant doctrinal literature was coming into the country. Actually, the Reformation was successful among all classes of the population. Many of the nobility supported it. The common people flocked by thousands to the cause. Of special importance in winning them were the plays, ballads, and pamphlets that blanketed the country. Lyrics on sacred themes taught doctrine, cast ridicule on the papacy, and provided a hymnody for the masses. Recent scholarship has shown that the rising middle class was also heavily involved. Students were constantly moving to and from centers of learning on the Continent, where they were introduced to the writings and ideas of Hus, Luther, Calvin, and others. John Knox himself said in his History[12] that "merchants and mariners" had a prominent role in bringing religious books and ideas from the mainland. Amazingly, all this Reformation development was going on when there were hardly any Protestant preachers in Scotland and not even a semblance of a church organization.

It should be remembered that after the death of James V (1542), Scotland was ruled by his wife, Mary of Guise, of a noble French family and virtually a tool of the French. Her daughter Mary, when six years old, was sent for education to France where she was married to the Dauphin, the crown prince Francis, son of Henry II and Catherine de Medici. For seventeen months (until December 1560) Mary Stuart was queen of France. Meanwhile, in an effort to maintain her position, Mary of Guise even had French troops stationed in Scotland. Many of the nobles, because they were both Protestants and good Scots, banded together to expel the French. Aided by an English fleet they defeated the French in 1560. In the midst of this conflict Mary of Guise

---

12. The fuller title is *History of the Reformation of Religion Within the Realm of Scotland*. In a polemical era characterized by very partisan literature that often distorted the truth, Knox's work stands out as a good piece of historical writing and a valuable source of information about the times.

died, and Scotland was without a ruling sovereign.

John Knox had returned to Scotland in 1559, and he set about to organize a reformation that already had become a reality. The Roman church had virtually ceased to function. Without waiting for the absent queen to express an opinion, Parliament approved the First Scottish Confession and established the Church of Scotland in August of 1560.

Mary Stuart came back to Scotland in 1561. From the outset, she experienced the opposition of Knox, whose outspoken denunciations destroyed the possibility of persuading her to moderate or forsake her Roman Catholicism. Her determination to restore Romanism in Scotland brought her many enemies. But her love affairs with worthless men sealed her downfall. The refusal of the nobles to permit her second husband, the Earl of Bothwell, to rule as king led to a military confrontation, her defeat, and her imprisonment in 1567. Mary abdicated in favor of her son James VI; and her half brother, the Earl of Moray, became regent. After Mary fled to England for safety and was imprisoned there, plots against Elizabeth I began to swirl around Mary's head. Finally, in 1587 Elizabeth was pressured into executing Mary.

Protestantism was firmly established by Parliament. Knox had done his work. His impress may still be seen on the Church of Scotland and the educational system of the land. When Knox died (1572), Andrew Melville took over the work and perfected the system Knox had established. Though Knox had tolerated the episcopal form of church government, Melville opposed it. And after a lengthy conflict between the episcopal and presbyterian systems, presbyterianism finally won out completely in 1690.

The Reformation in the Netherlands

The teachings of Luther and especially of Calvin were readily accepted in the Netherlands. And the great humanist Erasmus did much of his work there, writing devastating satires on the Roman church and other institutions of contemporary society under such titles as *The Praise of Folly* and *Familiar Colloquies*. Moreover, the Bible had been translated into Flemish several years before Luther was born. The Brethren of the Common Life were another important factor in the advancement of the Reformation in the Netherlands.

Spain controlled the Netherlands during the Reformation, and it was the great Charles V who first had to deal with Protestants. There were many martyrdoms in his days, especially of Anabaptists. Because Charles had been born in the Netherlands, the populace tended to put up with his policies. With his successor, Philip II (1556-1598), conditions radically changed however. To begin with he was looked upon as a Spanish foreigner in a day of rising nationalism in the Lowlands. Second, his autocratic ways were greatly resented by the more moderate Netherlanders. Third, his severe financial exactions threatened economic ruin of the fairly well-to-do burghers of the region. Fourth, Philip's introduction of the Inquisition and the stationing of the Duke of Alva and numerous Spanish troops in the Lowlands proved to be the last straw. Alva's "Council of Blood" is credited with executing well over six thousand Lowlanders. Thus there erupted an eighty-year war of independence, which evidently was not merely a struggle between Protestants and Roman Catholics. This is clear from the fact that in its early stages the Protestant north (Holland) and Roman Catholic south (Belgium) united to expel the hated Spaniard. Ultimately however, the Spanish were able to drive a wedge between the northern and southern provinces, and the Dutch fought on alone.

William of Orange led the Dutch patriots in resistance. Though the Dutch did not seem to be very successful on land, they did fairly well on the sea. There they had the help of a navy, which Elizabeth provided. Though William was assassinated in 1584, the Dutch were able to expel the last of the Spanish in 1609 and to win independence officially in 1648 with the Peace of Westphalia. The Reformed church was established as the state church of the Netherlands.

While still technically at war with Spain, the Dutch settled a colony at New Netherland (New York) in the 1620s and likewise moved into the East Indies to take over former Portuguese territory. They felt justified in occupying Portuguese holdings because Philip II had moved into Portugal and annexed both it and its empire. Subsequently they planted a settlement at the Cape of Good Hope as a halfway station between their homeland and their colonies in the Far East. Thus the Dutch Reformed church gained a foothold in North America, Africa, and Indonesia.

The Counter-Reformation

It is cogently argued that the term *Counter-Reformation* is misleading. The Roman Catholic church, like a sleeping giant, was not suddenly awakened to new life and vigor by the Protestant menace alone. Calls for reforming the teachings and practices of the church could be heard throughout the fifteenth century and earlier. And in some quarters reforms of sorts were undertaken long before Luther posted his theses at Wittenberg in 1517. But it is undeniably true that the threat of Protestant successes spurred the Roman church's efforts to set her house in order. And she did counterattack at numerous points to regain areas lost or in danger of being lost to Protestants.

The Roman church was successful in these efforts for many reasons, among which must be included the following: (1) As state churches were established in Protestant lands, the church increasingly came under the dominance of the political arm and was forced to serve the interests of the state. Thus Protestant churches began to suffer the same kind of fate as the Roman church had at the hands of a Francis I or Henry II of France. (2) The early evangelical enthusiasm declined, partly because of political involvements and partly because enthusiasm cannot be maintained at a high level for long. (3) A controversial spirit arose among Protestants—state-church people against dissenters, and divisiveness among members of the dominant group. (4) The papacy had the advantage of a thoroughly organized system. (5) The papacy was supported by Romance peoples— among whom there was little reformation. (6) The Roman church learned from the Reformation and set its house in order somewhat.

There were at least four aspects to the Counter-Reformation. The first of these was the Council of Trent. During Luther's ministry, there was constant agitation for and promise of a council to deal with the issues that the Reformation had raised. The Council of Trent was that council. It met in a total of twenty-five sessions, under three popes, from 1545 to 1563. The majority of participants came from Italy, Spain, France, and Germany. The council decided a host of issues, including the validity of the seven sacraments in bestowing merit on the believer and the necessity of some of them for salvation; the value of tradition as a basis of authority alongside the Bible; the canonicity of the apocryphal books of the Old Testament; the existence of purgatory; the value of images, relics, indulgences, and invocation of saints; and the importance of confession to a priest. It also defined more specifically the sacrificial aspects of the mass and decided that only the bread should be distributed to the laity. The council's work constituted a statement of faith by which a true Roman Catholic could determine his orthodoxy. No such comprehensive statement existed before. If it had, perhaps the force of the Reformation would have been blunted in some places.

The Inquisition was another feature of the Counter-Reformation. The medieval Inquisition, discussed earlier, was revived during the sixteenth century, especially in Italy and Spain and her dependencies. Though the Netherlands was subjected to a terrible persecution, Protestantism triumphed there. But in Italy, Spain, Portugal, and Belgium the Inquisition was fairly successful in extirpating the effects of the Reformation.

The Jesuits (Society of Jesus) were the third aspect of the Counter-Reformation. Founded in Paris in 1534 by Ignatius of Loyola (but officially recognized by Pope Paul III in 1540), the order demanded slavish obedience of all its members for the furtherance of the interests of the Roman church. They were absolutely unscrupulous in their methods, holding that it was permissible even to do evil if good might come of it. The Inquisition could win back individuals where the Reformation had slight effect. In other areas the Jesuits set up schools to convert the minds of the populace, sought to infiltrate governmental office, or used every means fair or foul to advance the cause of the church. Their power became so great and their methods so immoral that the order was suppressed by the papacy from 1773 to 1814 as a result of appeals from various governments.

It should be noted, however, that when Ignatius began his spiritual odyssey in 1521 and when he later launched the Society of Jesus, a counterattack against the Reformation was not in view. He himself was characterized by a missionary zeal and especially by a desire to convert Muslims. The three major goals of the Jesuits were to convert pagans, combat heresy, and promote education. Military features of the order derive from the fact that Ignatius had been a soldier before he decided to devote his life to the church.

A fourth aspect of the Counter-Reformation was a new and vigorous kind of spirituality that bloomed in a remarkable series of writings and movements. Some little spiritual books from this movement, such as the *Imitation of Christ* and the *Spiritual Exercises,* have received proper attention, but many have not. This new kind of devout life was characterized by a systematized examination of conscience, prayer, contemplation, and spiritual direction. Its roots lay deep in the Middle Ages with such groups as the Carthusians, who put special emphasis on the contemplative life and the practice of spiritual exercise. The *Devotio Moderna,* which made its appearance in the Low Countries during the fourteenth century, gave the movement greater impetus and was at the background of the Brethren and Sisters of the Common Life. In the same context fits the Italian Oratory of Divine Love. One can go on and on listing sixteenth century Italian or Spanish masters of spiritual cultivation. For instance there is the Italian Dominican Carioni, the Theatine Scupoli, the Spanish Dominican de Granada, and the writer de Cisneros. This magnificent and massive development deserves extensive new exploration for the benefit of contemporary lay movements. Though some of the developments noted here date earlier than the sixteenth century, it seems proper to include them. As noted above, there were signs of new life in Roman Catholicism before Martin Luther's attacks. Probably it is better to speak of a Roman Catholic Reformation than merely a Counter-Reformation.

The Thirty Years War

The Reformation period closed with a bloodbath that is known as the Thirty Years War. This conflict was really a combination of three antagonisms wrapped into one: Protestants versus Roman Catholics in Germany, emperor versus princes in the Holy Roman Empire, and France versus the Hapsburgs for the domination of Europe. The ambitions of other princes and states became involved; for example, Sweden and Brandenburg-Prussia.

The war is normally divided into four phases, with slightly varying dates and titles given to each:

1. Bohemian (1618-1623). At the background of this struggle is the fact that only Lutheranism had been recognized at the Peace of Augsburg in 1555, and Calvinism had rapidly advanced in the empire subsequently. In 1618 the Bohemians refused to recognize the newly elected Roman Catholic emperor, Ferdinand II, and elected Frederick V of the Palatinate of Germany, a Calvinist, as their king. This could only lead to open warfare. The imperial and Roman Catholic forces were victorious and crushed Protestantism in Bohemia, Moravia, Austria, and the Palatinate and engaged in a ruthless policy of reconversion and confiscation of Protestant property.

2. Danish (1623-1629). Christian IV of Denmark entered the struggle with English subsidies. Imperial and Roman Catholic forces were again victorious, and Protestantism in central Europe lay virtually prostrate.

3. Swedish (1630-1634). German princes, fearing the increasing power of the emperor, became involved in a squabble that weakened the imperial and Roman Catholic cause. At that point the great Gustavus Adolphus, "Lion of the North," landed an army in Germany. Evidently he believed he was fighting for the sake of the gospel, but he was at least equally interested in expanding the Swedish empire. For that reason some German Protestant princes were reluctant to join forces with him. Cardinal Richelieu of France (virtual prime minister) sought to use Gustavus's successes to weaken the power of the Spanish and Austrian Hapsburgs to the benefit of France and provided the Swedes with French subsidies. Gustavus won major victories, but was killed in battle in 1632; his army continued to fight.

4. International (1635-1648). The last phase of the war was a struggle for advantage by German states and foreign powers. Armies crossed and recrossed Germany, creating havoc and de-

struction. Finally, after years of negotiations the Peace of Westphalia was signed in 1648. Calvinism was recognized as as legal
religion along with Lutheranism and Roman Catholicism. Each
prince of the empire was permitted to determine the religion of
his state, according to the status of 1624. The Holy Roman Empire was further weakened by allowing the three hundred German political entities local autonomy. Holland and Switzerland
officially won independence. Sweden gained holdings in Germany. Brandenburg-Prussia expanded her territory. France won
Alsace and Lorraine from the Holy Roman Empire, which fact
raises a hint of future international conflict. Europe was now
officially divided religiously. England, Scotland, Holland, Scandinavia, part of Germany, and part of Switzerland had established
Protestant churches. The Roman church retained its hold everywhere else. Though Richelieu had restricted Huguenot power
and freedom in France, that significant minority clung to a degree of toleration for a few more decades.

In reply to those who criticize Christianity for the many wars it
presumably fought during the Reformation period, it must be
observed that in every case the political, economic, and social
considerations were often as important as the religious. Much of
the time, there was no clear-cut struggle between Roman Catholics and Protestants. Let it be remembered that both Protestants
and Roman Catholics were found in the armies that opposed
Mary Queen of Scots. The Reformer Henry of Navarre was supported in his bid for the throne of France both by Protestants and
Roman Catholics. And during much of the Thirty Years War,
Roman Catholic France was allied with Protestant Sweden.

7

Europe in the Modern Era

The Seventeenth Century

The seventeenth century was a century of orthodoxy. It was a time during which both Protestantism and Roman Catholicism were concerned with dogmatic formulation of their positions for the purpose of catechizing their adherents. Although some of this orthodoxy stressed Christian experience, much of it emphasized right thinking. The drying up of the wellsprings of vitality in religion had started by the beginning of the seventeenth century, but the process was hastened in certain areas of Europe that lay prostrate as a result of the Thirty Years War. Cold orthodoxy will not long satisfy. It will produce as least three reactions or results: rationalism, biblical revivalism, or extreme forms of mysticism. In other words, some will turn from ineffective supernatural Christianity to a religion based on human reason; others will return to a healthy combination of doctrine and experience; still others will substitute the authority of experience for the authority of creeds, catechisms, and sometimes Scripture itself.

Prominent among the inner light or mystical groups of the seventeenth century were the Quakers. The originator of the movement was George Fox of Drayton, England. Following a religious experience in 1646, he began a forty-year ministry of itinerant preaching. Quakerism spread very rapidly across England and, after its organization in 1660, to the Continent, Asia, Africa, the West Indies, and North America. There William Penn founded a haven for them in Pennsylvania in 1682, after it had become evident that New Jersey would not offer them adequate protection. The Quakers were severely persecuted, not only because of their great difference from the confessional churches on many points, but because of their open criticism of others. Quakers emphasized the work of the Holy Spirit: that the revelations of the Spirit, or the inner light, were equal to the Bible, but not contradictory to it; that since the Holy Spirit speaks to all, special training and ministers were unnecessary; that the Spirit could speak through women as well as men, and therefore they could teach and preach on an equal basis with men; and that formal worship was an abomination to God. They insisted on complete separation of church and state and did not practice the sacraments, take oaths, or do military service.

Their frequent imprisonments acquainted them with conditions in English jails and led them into prison reform. Later they launched a campaign against slavery and entered other forms of social service. In more recent times many Quakers have abandoned the traditional service, in which people sat silently until "moved by the Spirit" to share with those gathered, and have turned to a simple service led by a pastor. There are well over 200,000 Quakers (or Friends) in the world today, of which about 125,000 live in the United States and 40,000 in Kenya.

The teachings of the Swedish scientist Emanuel Swedenborg (1688-1772) led to the founding of the New Jerusalem Church. He claimed to have had a revelation that enabled him to communicate with the world of spirits and angels; and during his various communications with that world, he claimed to have learned the secrets of the universe. Instead of rejecting the Bible, he spiritualized or allegorized it. The theological system he developed had some similarities to Gnosticism. He seems to have denied the Trinity, original sin, the vicarious atonement, and the bodily resurrection. But some individual congregations of the New Jerusalem Church do not appear to be quite so unorthodox. Actually,

Robert Hindmarsh launched the New Jerusalem Church in London in the 1780s. Swedenborgian churches were established mainly in England, Sweden, Germany, and North America. Membership in the New Jerusalem Church worldwide has shrunk to 3,727, of which 2,568 live in the United States, according to a current report from the church's headquarters.

Within Romanism also there was a reaction to the rationalization of dogma, which reaction expressed itself in an extreme mystical movement. Known as Quietism, it held that God can act on man to meet his spiritual need only as man surrenders himself utterly. When man's soul is completely passive, the way is open to receive impartation of divine light from God. Some of the Quietists were pantheistic in approach, teaching that contemplation of the Divine would lead to absorption into the Divine. Michael Molinos in Spain and Madame Guyon and Francis Fénelon in France were three of Quietism's leading writers. Recognizing that Quietism seemed to need none of the externalities of the Roman church and that it was therefore a danger to the system, the Jesuits mounted an effective assault on the movement, first in Spain and then in France.

A contemporary Roman Catholic reaction that stressed experience, though not of the same type, was Jansenism. So named for its leader Cornelis Jansen, it sought to return to the teachings of Augustine and to stress greater personal holiness and the necessity of divine grace for conversion. As a reform movement, Jansenism attracted numerous outstanding scholars, among them Blaise Pascal. The Jesuits launched a violent attack on the Jansenists, and Pope Innocent X condemned their teachings in a papal bull in 1653. Louis XIV, also engaged in some controversy with the papacy, defended the Jansenists. But the Jesuits continued the attack, and in 1713 Pope Clement XI issued another papal bull against them, this time condemning 101 statements from one of their writings—many of them direct quotations from St. Augustine.

A seventeenth-century evangelical corrective to the cold orthodoxy of the Lutheran church was Pietism. Although its main center was in Germany, it claimed many adherents in Switzerland and Holland as well. In Holland, the revolt was against the

Dutch Reformed church. Pietism emphasized the need for a regeneration experience on the part of all, promoted a living Christianity wherein the love of God would be expressed, and encouraged practical church work and Bible study on the part of laymen. The great leaders of German Pietism were P. J. Spener and A. H. Francke; the latter was especially important for his training schools and institutions for the needy at Halle (e.g., an orphanage, a hospital, a widows' home). Spener and Francke did not want to found a new church but only to form evangelical groups within the established Lutheran church to leaven the larger community. Its lack of organization made it somewhat ineffective in perpetuating its message and ministry, however. And the almost pharisaical attitudes and austere legalism of many of its adherents did not provide the winsome attractiveness to a more elevated Christianity that Spener and Francke had desired.

Although Pietism reacted primarily against Lutheranism, Arminianism reacted against the Reformed church of Holland. Calvinism in Holland had grown much more harsh and severe than it was in Calvin's day; so the Arminians in 1610 (a year after the death of Jacobus Arminius, their leader) addressed a *Remonstrance* to the states of Holland. In it they emphasized the opportunity and responsibility of man in salvation: that man faces a choice of salvation or condemnation and is actually free, that predestination is conditioned on God's foreknowledge of man's faith and perseverance, that although grace is indispensable it is not irresistible, and that to stay saved man must desire God's help and be actively engaged in living the Christian life. Perhaps it should be noted that both Arminianism and Calvinism have over the centuries grown more extreme than the views set forth by their founders. Much misunderstanding of both positions and much quibbling between groups holding these divergent positions could be stopped if there were a wider reading and understanding of the works of Calvin and Arminius. At any rate the Dutch church did not welcome the Arminian *Remonstrance*, but at the Synod of Dort in 1618 set forth the five points of Calvinism in response to it: total depravity of man after the Fall, unconditional election, limited atonement, irresistible grace (divine grace cannot be rejected by the elect), and perseverance of the saints (they cannot fall from grace).

One of the more important rationalistic movements of the seventeenth century was Socinianism, so named for its founder, Faustus Socinus (1539-1604). Originally from Italy, Socinus spent most of his years of teaching and preaching in Poland. There he espoused an essentially anti-Trinitarian system, a rationalistic interpretation of Scripture, and separation of church and state. He taught that Christ was a man who lived a life of exemplary obedience and who ultimately was deified. One becomes a Christian by following Christ's example of devotion to God, renunciation of the world, and humility. Christ's death was not substitutionary, but merely an example of ultimate devotion. After a couple of generations of success in Poland, the Socinian movement was broken up by the Jesuits, and its followers were banished. Many found their way to Holland, where they were welcomed by Arminians and others and where they injected a considerable liberal influence into the theology of the country. Some went to England, where they also joined with Arminians to infuse Anglicanism with a liberalizing tendency.

The Eighteenth Century

If the seventeenth century was the age of orthodoxy, the eighteenth was the age of rationalism. In part, rationalism was a reaction to or an outgrowth of cold orthodoxy. And in part it grew out of the great emphasis on faith and emotion during the seventeenth century. Many of the groups that stressed experience did not strive hard enough to meet the intellectual needs of their constituency. In their emphasis on emotion, they neglected a doctrinal basis of their faith. Note for instance that Immanuel Kant, a watershed in the history of philosophy, was the son of Pietistic parents and that he was educated as a Pietist until 1740. The rise of rationalism also resulted from the place given to philosophy in the universities. During the Middle Ages philosophy and theology had been wed in the system called Scholasticism; but with the decline of Scholasticism and the church the two were divorced, with the result that philosophy became an enemy of theology.

Furthermore, the rise of rationalism was fostered by scientific developments. Copernicus (1473-1543) was responsible for developing the view that the sun instead of the earth was the center of the universe. Galileo (1564-1642) trained the telescope on the heavens and used observation to support Copernicus's view of the solar system. Descartes (1596-1650) propounded the concept of a universe governed by natural law, and Isaac Newton (1642-1727) furnished the principle that the law of gravity held the universe together and caused it to function as it did. In another connection Descartes taught that one ought never to allow himself to be persuaded of the truth of anything unless on the evidence of his reason. And Francis Bacon (1561-1626) introduced the inductive method, according to which a scientist accepted nothing on the basis of authority alone, but developed his theories by observing phenomena. So knowledge was tied to what the senses could discover and what the reason could deduce. Revelation tended to take a back seat to reason and to knowledge gained by sense perception.

The new scientific developments led to the view that the universe was a closed system of cause and effect, ruled by universal and dependable laws. God was considered to be a necessary first cause to start the system going; but once He set the universe in motion, He no longer interfered with its natural processes. Miracle, providence, prayer, and revelation were ruled out. The natural religion of deism took over. God was still viewed as Creator, but He had little to do with the universe, which He as a kind of watchmaker had wound up and let run according to natural laws. Since He did not interfere in this universe, there was no such thing as revelation. Thus the Bible was a human book with some elevated ethical principles and spiritual lessons that had value for humanity. Jesus was only a human with an amazing God-consciousness and a superior ethic to be emulated. Deism made great inroads in England, France, Germany, and other countries of Europe, as well as in America.

From the same context as deism rose a new social philosophy whose proponents included John Locke and the philosophes, or social philosophers. Locke (1632-1704) taught that just as the universe was governed by natural law, so men (as part of nature) were guaranteed certain natural rights. His political philosophy was an important facet of the political theory of the eighteenth century and was written into the American Declaration of Independence and the French Declaration of the Rights of Man. His religious views were significant too. In *An Essay Concerning Toleration, The Reasonableness of Christianity,* and in his four letters on toleration he argued that no one could be saved by a religion that was forced upon him and that he did not believe. Therefore, he called for religious toleration and the separation of church and state.

The philosophes, a group of middle class French intellectuals of the eighteenth century, broadened Locke's views and popularized them in France. Voltaire ("prince of the philosophes"), Diderot, and others taught that just as the universe was governed by natural law, so society was governed by natural laws. And just as men could discover the laws of nature and bend it to the service of mankind, so men could discover the laws of society and make it a more equitable and reasonable structure. In doing so, they held that the institutions of the past, or "debris," which had impeded man's progress, had to go. One of the most important of these restrictive institutions was the church. And the church in France, home of the philosphes and of the Enlightenment, was the Roman Catholic church. Thus began open warfare between "science" and theology in the West. Voltaire and other leaders of the Enlightenment were vocal in their opposition to the church and the orthodox view of the Bible. Voltaire (1694-1778) in his *Questions of Dr. Zapata* helped to lay the foundation for rationalistic higher criticism of the Bible. What began in the eighteenth century developed into a formal system of biblical criticism late in the nineteenth century.

Attack and counterattack are characteristic both of the eighteenth and nineteenth centuries. Forces at work during the nineteenth century will be discussed later. The attack during the eighteenth century was launched by rationalism; a counterattack by such groups as Moravians and Methodists. The Moravian movement was an outgrowth of Pietism. Its leader, Count Nikolaus von Zinzendorf, had spent several years in one of the Pietist schools at Halle. In 1722 Zinzendorf invited exiled Protestants from Bohemia and Moravia to settle on his estate in Saxony, where they organized as the "renewed fraternity." Zinzendorf himself developed a very keen interest in world evangelization, but he was especially concerned with establishing an international fellowship of true believers belonging to various religious bodies. Therefore he did not want to start a new denomination. His own colony he kept within the Lutheran church.

As Moravian missionaries became active in preaching the gospel and in organizing groups of believers within the established churches of Europe, they had great success in founding fellowships in Holland, Denmark, England, Switzerland, North America, and elsewhere in Germany. When Zinzendorf fell into the disfavor of the Lutheran church and hence the Saxon government, he was exiled for over ten years. During those years, much against his will, the Moravians organized as a separate denomination known as the Unity of the Brethren (1742), and won recognition from the Saxon government. In England they became known as Moravians. Their doctrinal position was basically that of the Lutheran Augsburg Confession.

The Moravians had a direct influence on the establishment of the Methodist movement, which was founded by John and Charles Wesley and George Whitefield. Moravian missionaries exposed the Wesleys to the gospel message while the latter were on a fruitless missionary journey to the New World and had not yet been converted. Later, another Moravian, Peter Boehler, brought the Wesleys to Christ. Shortly thereafter, John Wesley visited Zinzendorf in Germany and then embarked on his lifework. *Methodist* was the name applied to the "holy club" at Oxford to which the Wesleys and George Whitefield had belonged; subsequently it passed on to the movement begun by the three. John Wesley (1703-1791) and George Whitefield (1714-1770) were the great preachers; Charles Wesley (1708-1788) was the hymn writer. Having composed some 7,270 hymns, he is ranked by many as the greatest hymn writer of all ages.[1] As the Wesleys carried on their revival efforts they received little en-

---

1. Charles Wesley was contemporary with another great hymn writer, Isaac Watts (1674-1748). John Newton (1725-1807) began his hymn-writing ministry as Wesley was passing off the scene.

couragement from the Anglican church, of which they were members. Shut out of many Anglican churches, they took a cue from Whitefield, who had had great success in outdoor preaching in America. Tremendous crowds constantly gathered for their meetings.

Early Methodism was characterized by the preaching of present assurance of salvation, development of the inner spiritual life, belief in the attainability of Christian perfection in this life, and a dignified ritual. The Wesleys were Arminian in their theology, but Whitefield was Calvinistic. Originally, John Wesley did not wish to organize the Methodist church as a separate denomination; he set up societies within the Anglican church. But conditions in America demanded a separation, and the Methodist Episcopal church was established in 1784. In England, Methodism separated from the Anglican church about the same time.

As well as having a wide spiritual impact, Methodism proved to be a very real answer to the social ills of the day. Spiritually, Methodism was the answer to deism in England, especially among the lower and middle classes. And it met the needs of the new laboring classes in the cities, for whom the Anglican church did not assume much responsibility. Socially, in large measure it retarded forces that in France led to revolution: it provided medical dispensaries, orphanages, and relief for the poor; it stood at the front of the movement for prison reform, the abolition of slavery, and the regulation of industry.[2]

The Nineteenth Century

If the seventeenth century may be characterized as the age of orthodoxy and the eighteenth as the age of rationalism, the nineteenth may be characterized as the age of science. But science took over after about the middle of the century; other forces were at work in the early part of the century. The Enlightenment of the eighteenth century had gone too far in its rationalism and

2. The significance of Methodism for English social and political development is detailed in J. Wesley Bready's *This Freedom Whence?* and *England Before and After Wesley*. Though these books have been attacked, much of what they say about the contributions of Methodism is valid. The latter is especially useful.

in its effort to eradicate religion and remove feeling from all of life. The first part of the nineteenth century saw in Romanticism a reaction to that extreme.

Romanticism was characterized by a new emphasis on feeling, faith, individualism, and communion with nature divine and untamed. There was a new emphasis on feeling in all phases of life—music, poetry, drama, and certainly religion. Faith—not necessarily orthodox faith—was considered to be good. Individualism manifested itself in a new impatience with society's laws and rules of conduct and sought expression in personal religion and individualized education. Moreover, there was a new emphasis on the organic view of history and society. That is, it was felt that the present must be understood in connection with the past and the future; and that there is slow, not radical, development of the social organism. This intellectual context is important for the appearance and impact of Darwinian thought.

One facet of the Romantic reaction was the revival of religion of all types. Some took the aesthetic approach and found a delight in vesture and symbol and stained glass and stately organ music. Others turned from rationalistic apologies for Christianity to emotional experience of a more or less orthodox faith. Napoleon made a concordat with the papacy (1801) and restored the Roman Catholic church in France. Schleiermacher, in Germany, redefined religion as feeling—man's feeling of dependence on God as he comes to realize how finite, limited, and temporary he is in comparison with the eternal principle indwelling the world. Schleiermacher's rationalized Christianity has influenced such recent movements as neo-orthodoxy and existentialism.

An evangelical revival moved through the Church of England during the first third of the century under the leadership of such well-known saints as John Newton and William Wilberforce.[3] Meanwhile Methodist, Baptist, and other dissenter groups grew rapidly in number. The Sunday school movement spread across England like a prairie fire, and several Bible societies were

3. This evangelical party is known as the Low Church party. There is in the Anglican church also a High Church party, Anglo-Catholic in sentiment, and the Broad Church party, which seeks to take the middle way of compromise and make Anglicanism the church of the nation.

founded in Europe and America, including the British and Foreign Bible Society, the Berlin Bible Society, and the American Bible Society. At the same time, the foreign missions movement continued to expand. In fact the nineteenth century has been called the "Great Century of Protestant Missions."

The modern missionary movement began with William Carey (1761-1834), whose efforts led to the founding of the Baptist Missionary Society at Kettering, England, in 1792. The following year Carey set out for India. As reports of his work reached home, members of other denominations banded together to form the London Missionary Society (1795). Other societies followed in rapid succession. Carey taught himself several languages of India and became a leader in Bible translation. He was followed there by the Anglican Henry Martyn and the Church of Scotland's Alexander Duff. Samuel Marsden pioneered for over forty years in Australia, New Zealand, and the Pacific Islands. The London Missionary Society sent Robert Morrison to open up the work in China, and Robert and Mary Moffat and their son-in-law, David Livingstone, to Africa. Morrison provided a Chinese dictionary and a Chinese translation of the Bible for later missionaries there. Moffat translated the Bible into important tribal languages of South Africa. Livingstone opened up central Africa. In 1865 J. Hudson Taylor founded the China Inland Mission, one of the great interdenominational faith missions. His writings and extensive travels led to the establishment of several other faith missions.

England and Scotland were not the only European countries sending out missionaries during the nineteenth century. In 1821 the Basel Evangelical Missionary Society and the Danish Missionary Society were founded. Three years later, in 1824, the Berlin Missionary Society and the Paris Missionary Society came into being.

Although the beginnings of the scientific revolution can be traced to the sixteenth century, science did not make its full impact on society until the nineteenth century. It was the harnessing of technology and science that drastically changed the way men lived. Though the factory system began to reshape the English countryside and herd masses of humanity into foreboding aggregations called cities during the late eighteenth century, the industrial revolution was not so widespread in other countries until the nineteenth century. About the middle of the century, the rapidity of new technological breakthroughs started to accelerate. The rubber and petroleum industries began to develop about that time. New technological improvements resulted in the lowering of the price of steel by one-half between 1856 and 1870. New alloys and synthetic fabrics joined the long list of developments that suddenly changed human existence and speeded up the growth of cities.

As people moved into the cities, they found their lives to be hard indeed. Whole familes worked for pittances from dawn to dark in factories without safety devices, and they lived in impossible tenements. They were reduced to concentrating all their energies on making their livings—on keeping bodies and souls together. Increasingly their interests were centered in organizations that would better their way of life. As unions and governmental agencies took over functions and provided social outlets previously furnished by the church, society became increasingly secularized. Materialism overspread all things. Sunday was the workers' day off, and they used it as a day for recreation. In many cities, had they wanted to go to church there would not have been enough churches for them to attend, because denominations often failed to keep up with the need. It may be said that the real enemy of religion was the science of the shop rather than the science of the laboratory.

Yet the impact of the science of the laboratory was tremendous. The publication of Darwin's *Origin of Species* (1859) and *The Descent of Man* (1871) culminated a long history of increasing acceptance of the concept of evolution in the natural sciences. In the hands of its popularizers (Thomas Huxley, Ernst Haeckel, and others) Darwin's teachings were somewhat modified and became widely accepted. Man was no longer viewed as the creature of God, but as the product of an infinite process of development necessitated by the demands of environment. Creative intelligence had been banished from the universe; there was no longer any need for God. The reaction of established religion to Darwinism was threefold: some capitulated and turned their backs on Christianity; other repudiated the claims of science; the majority worked out some sort of compromise between their faith and the new science. The struggle was especially vehement because at the time Darwin's publications hit English bookstores the country was largely controlled by adherents of a biblical orthodoxy that interpreted the Bible literally.

Not only did the concept of evolution invade the fields of the natural sciences, cultural interpretation, and social theory, but it invaded the field of religion as well. That man started out with no religion and finally advanced to the elevated viewpoint of monotheism was commonly taught. The Bible was not a product of revelation, but a collection of myths, legends, and a few historical facts; this collection developed over the years and finally was edited and put in the form we now know it. The Tübingen and Wellhausen schools of thought were two of those that subscribed to the evolutionary and higher critical viewpoint in religion. The German biblical critic Julius Wellhausen (1844-1918) was a pivotal figure in the rise of liberal scholarship. His *Prolegomena to the History of Israel* (1878) gave him a place in biblical studies considered by many comparable to that of Darwin in biology. Building on a long development in German scholarship, he denied Mosaic authorship of the Pentateuch and concluded that it was postexilic. The Old Testament, he believed, was put together by later editors using a variety of source materials. He applied to religion and the Old Testament the same evolutionary principles that Darwin and others were applying to the natural sciences. The system he constructed was destined to have impact worldwide during the twentieth century.

But while industrialism, antisupernaturalistic science, theological liberalism, and spiritual indifference made great inroads against Christianity during the nineteenth century, opposition forces were at work also. The Roman church asserted itself under the leadership of Pius IX (1846-1878), who issued the Syllabus of Errors (1864) and called the first Vatican Council (1870). The former condemned almost all the tendencies of the age, including pantheism, naturalism, rationalism, socialism, and Communism. The latter declared the dogma of papal infallibility, which extended to official pronouncements of the pope on faith and morals.

Attacking higher criticism were such scholars as E. W. Hengstenberg and Franz Delitzsch in Germany and Abraham Kuyper in Holland. The latter founded the Free University of Amsterdam, destined to become a great center of orthodoxy. To meet new social and religious conditions brought on by the industrial revolution, William Booth organized the Salvation Army, George Williams started the YMCA, and the Anglican church launched the Church Army. New mass evangelism efforts of D. L. Moody and Ira Sankey and others sought to reach the unchurched masses that had come to inhabit the cities. No longer was it true—as was the case in rural society—that people were in some way related to a local parish church. In short, throughout Western Europe there were individuals and groups who landed telling blows on behalf of biblical Christianity. And it would take pages to list the Spirit-sent revivals that fell on England and the Continent during the century.

8

The Church in America

The Seventeenth Century and Before

When Columbus sailed westward in 1492, he was not merely looking for a new route to the Indies. He hoped to discover new sources of wealth to finance another Crusade against the Muslims and to link up with leaders of the Far East to establish a massive pincers movement against the Muslim Middle East. Moreover, when he came upon the heathen tribes of the New World, his religious inclinations predominated again. He and Ferdinand agreed that measures should be taken to protect, convert, and civilize the Indians. Promptly, Spanish priests were sent out with the explorers and conquerors. A bishopric was established at Santo Domingo in 1512, another in Cuba in 1522, with others following in rapid succession. The University of Mexico and the University of San Marcos, in Lima, were both founded in 1551; others were built elsewhere in Latin America as the need arose. When one recalls that the Spanish sent their sons back to Europe for education, it will be clear that these New World institutions were primarily for the civilization of the natives. Admittedly, the Spanish oppressed and maltreated the Indians over the centuries, but it is nevertheless true that the church and crown made sincere and expensive moves to protect the natives. Shortly after the death of Luther, the Spanish settled Florida and then advanced into New Mexico and Texas. They were establishing their missions in California while Jefferson was writing the Declaration of Independence. Portuguese settlement in Brazil began in 1532, and of course the Roman church was established there. Thus, all of Latin America and part of the present area of the United States responded to the religious efforts of Spanish and Portuguese priests.

Although the French became interested in North America very early, they were not able to establish a permanent colony until 1608—at Quebec. Thereafter, French explorers and missionaries ranged across the northern part of the continent and throughout the Mississippi valley down to its mouth in Louisiana. They set up mission stations, trading posts, and forts wherever they penetrated, and established friendship with many Indian tribes. But the paucity of French settlers in the New World, inadequate colonial policies, and the defeat of French forces ultimately brought an end to the French Empire in North America and the effects of French Jesuit work everywhere except in Quebec and Louisiana.

At Jamestown in 1607, the English established their first successful colony. Planted by the Virginia Company, the colony was basically an economic venture; but the Anglican church was established there to meet the spiritual needs of the colonists, who were members of the Church of England. About the same time, a group of Pilgrim separatists, persecuted in England because of their religious views, took refuge in Holland. Finally they made arrangements with the London Company to settle in Virginia. But the *Mayflower* and the Pilgrims landed at Plymouth, Massachusetts, instead, introducing Congregationalism to New England in 1620.

A decade later the Massachusetts Bay company came with its charter, stockholders, and board of directors to plant colonies at Salem, Boston, and the immediate vicinity. These Puritans sought to escape the despotism of Charles I and to found a "wilderness Zion," but economic reasons for colonization were much greater than religious historians often have been willing to admit. Like the Pilgrims the Puritans were Calvinistic in doctrine;

and they ultimately also accepted the congregational form of government. In 1691 the Pilgrim and Puritan settlements amalgamated to form Massachusetts, and Maine was included as part of the union until it became a state in 1820.

Meanwhile, primarily because of economic advantage, settlers of a Congregational conviction spilled over into Connecticut on the south and New Hampshire and Vermont on the north. Separatists like Roger Williams moved to Rhode Island, where Baptist churches were first organized on North American shores and where separation of church and state was practiced in an atmosphere of almost complete religious liberty.

Both Puritans and Anglicans were interested in an educated ministry and founded colleges for that purpose. In 1636 and 1701 respectively, the Puritans launched Harvard and Yale. In 1693, the Anglicans chartered William and Mary in Williamsburg. Because denser population in towns permitted it, the New Englanders also built public elementary and secondary schools to provide religious instruction for the populace and to train them for intelligent citizenship. The Middle Colonies organized parochial schools for similar reasons.

About the time Massachusetts settlers were spilling over into Connecticut (1630s), Lord Baltimore was planting a colony in Maryland. Although Baltimore designed his colony as a haven for persecuted Roman Catholics, not too many came, even on the first boatloads of settlers. Therefore, in order to maintain a successful economic venture and to protect Roman Catholics against an unsympathetic Protestant majority, he permitted religious toleration. Puritans came to Maryland in large numbers, but Anglicanism was established at the end of the century, when Maryland became a royal colony.

Because Quakers were persecuted in both England and New England, William Penn sought to provide a haven for them in Pennsylvania during the last decades of the seventeenth century. And because Quakerism did not lend itself to exclusiveness and because Penn wanted a profitable colony, the doors were thrown open to all who would come. Penn advertised widely in Europe with good success, and Germans came in droves to Penn's Woods. There were Lutherans, Moravians, and a host of German sects. West Jersey, too, became a Quaker settlement.

In 1623 New Amsterdam was founded on Manhattan Island. Although the Dutch did not profess any religious motivation for colonization, they naturally favored the Reformed church, the first of which appeared in 1628. New York developed a cosmopolitan character, however, and the efforts of Dutch governors to enforce religious conformity were never successful. After the English took over New Netherland, they established the Anglican church there in 1693—at least in New York City and surrounding counties. Lutherans settled in New Amsterdam almost as soon as the Dutch Reformed, but they did not fare very well under Dutch rule. The Lutherans were more successful, however, in the Swedish colony on the Delaware, planted in 1638. This too fell into the hands of the Dutch and finally into the hands of the English. The first permanent English Presbyterian church was also established in New Netherland—on Long Island in 1640. But in the early days the Presbyterians were most numerous in East Jersey and Pennsylvania. Religious developments in the Carolinas were somewhat uncertain in the early days. The proprietors, who received their grant in 1663, gave considerable freedom to settlers, who had spilled over the border into North Carolina from Virginia and who came into South Carolina in considerable numbers from the West Indies.

The Eighteenth Century

The development of the colonies south of Virginia occurred largely in the eighteenth century. In fact, settlement in Georgia did not even begin until 1733. In all these colonies the Anglican church ultimately became the established church. It was established in South Carolina in 1706, Georgia in 1758, and North Carolina in 1765. The eighteenth century was also a time when the Anglican church made a determined effort to reorganize and to improve ministers, morals, and service rendered in the parishes. The famous Society for the Propagation of the Gospel in Foreign Parts took the lead in this effort.

In general it may be said that at the time of the American Revolution the Anglican church dominated the Southern Colonies and the Congregational church the Northern Colonies, while in the Middle Colonies there was diversity. To be more specific, the Anglican church was the established church in Georgia, South Carolina, North Carolina, Virginia, Maryland, and New York City and surrounding counties. The Congregational church was established in Massachusetts (Maine), Connecticut, and New Hampshire. In New Jersey, Pennsylvania, Delaware, and Rhode Island there was no state church.

It is remarkable that although in the rest of the Western world before, during, and after the American Revolution a state church was everywhere established, in the United States complete separation of church and state was achieved in most states, with the accompanying disestablishment of the church. Perhaps it should be noted that an established church is one officially maintained by a government and supported by taxes levied on all citizens. The degree of toleration accorded to minority faiths varies from place to place.

DISESTABLISHMENT OF THE CHURCHES

There are several reasons for the disestablishment of the church in the United States. First, the kind and extent of immigration that flowed into the colonies after 1690 was significant. It brought about such a mixture of peoples and faiths that ultimately a majority faith existed almost nowhere. First came Quakers and some Huguenots. Quakers settled mainly in Pennsylvania and dominated the colony; their opposition to formal church structure prevented the rise of a state church there. Quaker presence in New Jersey contributed to the religious mixture in that colony, and Pennsylvania's control over Delaware during most of the colonial period insured freedom of religion there. Huguenots found refuge in several colonies. Having suffered from persecution in France, they had no desire to persecute others. The second great wave of immigrants, about 1700, consisted of some two hundred thousand Germans. Though a great percentage of these were Lutheran and Reformed, many smaller sects were represented; and of the total, most were dominated by the Pietistic emphasis on inner, personal religion. Such persons had no desire to dominate the religious expression of others. The Germans went in large numbers to Pennsylvania and northern New York. Last came a wave of about two hundred fifty thousand Scotch-Irish from northern Ireland—Presbyterians who had been persecuted by the Anglican church there. They spread widely over the Middle and Southern colonies, especially along the back valley of the Appalachians, and contributed greatly to religious diversity. By 1760 there were about 2.5 million people in the colonies, of which about one-third were foreign born.

A second influence favoring disestablishment was the effect of the proprietary colonies. All the colonies established after 1660 were proprietary grants. Something already has been said about the fact that a desire for a successful colonial venture led to religious toleration in Pennsylvania, and especially Maryland. The same was true for New York, Georgia, North and South Carolina, New Jersey, and Delaware, all of which were proprietary colonies at one time. During periods when these colonies were under proprietary control, religious pluralism increased. And even though a state church might have been imposed later, it could not forever endure, because the population was too religiously diverse.

Third, the leveling influence of the great revivals that shook the colonies during the eighteenth century made their impact. The revivals transcended denominational lines, and the revivalists stressed the equality of all men in the sight of God.

Fourth, pioneering attitudes made a contribution similar to that of the revivals. The frontier was a leveler. Moreover, the pioneer had to become a self-reliant individualist if he was to survive. Individualism and religious institutionalism did not mix well. Frontiersmen generally have been suspicious of or opposed to the establishment or the more settled areas (in the United States, the East).

Fifth, the impact of the unchurched was significant. Because the frontier moved so fast and people were spread out in such a thin line, the churches failed to keep up with the needs of the population. Many people were without church membership—in proportion to the population, probably more than anywhere else in Christendom during the first third of the eighteenth century.

The unchurched do not have much interest in supporting an established religion.

Sixth, natural rights philosophy influenced many. Something was said in the last chapter about natural rights philosophy and the rise of deism during the eighteenth century. One of the rights educated men of that day came to accept was the privilege of deciding the kind of religious belief they should follow. John Locke in his *Letters on Toleration* (1689-1706) had argued for the separation of church and state and for the voluntary nature of one's religious affiliation. Many leaders of the American Revolutionary generation, such as Jefferson, were greatly imbued with this philosophy, and they were active in bringing down the church establishment in Virginia soon after the new nation won its independence.

It should be added that when the Revolution began the Anglican church suffered greatly. Many ministers were loyalist in sympathies and left their churches either by choice or because of intimidation. So did many of their parishioners, for that matter, as the Church of England, the Anglican church, took the brunt of attack from patriot opponents. When the war was over, there were few Anglican ministers left in the country and many churches had been destroyed. Especially in the states south of Virginia the Anglican church had little support, and disestablishment was not difficult there.

Last, agitation for the appointment of an Anglican bishop in America, especially on the part of the Society for the Propagation of the Gospel, stirred fires of disestablishment. Cries of dismay rose from the influential Congregational and Presbyterian camps. And coming as it did when the colonists increasingly resented the rule of Parliament, this proposal stirred political opposition as well as religious. If Parliament could establish religion in all the colonies, it could by so much tighten the noose around the necks of a people looking for greater freedom.

Thus it may be seen that disestablishment was almost a foregone conclusion in the United States. With the founding of the new nation, one after another the edifices of state church establishment toppled. The last to go was Congregationalism: in New Hampshire, 1817; Connecticut, 1818; and Massachusetts, 1833.

THE CHURCHES AND THE REVOLUTION

If there was so much religious diversity and agitation during the eighteenth century, it may be well to ask about the attitudes of the various denominations toward the Revolution and their participation in it. The Anglicans were divided, with a probable loyalist majority. In the North they were generally loyalist; but in the South many of the great planters, among them Washington, favored the Revolutionary cause. The Congregationalists gave enthusiastic support, their ministers preaching sermons in favor of the patriot cause. The Presbyterians were generally patriot, their struggle with royal governors and the Anglican church in the colonies being something of a continuation of the Presbyterian-Anglican conflict in England. One of the greatest Presbyterian patriots was John Witherspoon, signer of the Articles of Confederation and the only clergyman to sign the Declaration of Independence. Lutherans also enthusiastically supported the Revolution, especially under the leadership of the Muhlenbergs. Though divided, the Roman Catholics generally were patriot. The Baptists supported the Revolution because, for one thing, they felt that the cause of separation of church and state was at stake. They believed that British victory would bring new political controls and a new religious tightening, accompanied by the installation of an Anglican bishop in America. It should be noted, however, that some Baptists, like some Congregationalists and Presbyterians, were reticent about committing themselves to the patriot cause. Methodists were suspect because Wesley at the beginning of the war urged neutrality, but native-born preachers seem to have been in sympathy with the Revolution. Although Quakers, Mennonites, and Moravians were conscientious objectors, a large percentage of them were in sympathy with the Revolution and some even joined the army.

The Revolution brought about the dissolution of ties between many religious bodies in America and Europe, necessitating separate organization in America. For other reasons some groups likewise organized. William White and Samuel Seabury, Jr., were responsible for rehabilitating the Anglican church after the war; and it was organized as the Protestant Episcopal Church in 1789, along more democratic lines than the Church of England. Cut loose from English Methodism by the force of circumstances, the Methodists organized in 1784 as the Methodist Episcopal Church, under the leadership of Francis Asbury. In the same year, American Roman Catholic dependence on British jurisdiction terminated, and in 1789 John Carroll became the first Roman Catholic bishop, with Baltimore as his see. The Baptists formed a General Committee in 1784. And the Presbyterians were in Philadelphia drawing up a constitution for their church at the same time as the national Constitution was being formed in 1787.

THE GREAT AWAKENING

One of the major events of American Christianity during the eighteenth century was the Great Awakening. With the loss of the evangelical enthusiasm that characterized the first generation of Congregationalists, Presbyterians, and others, and with the increase of the unchurched on the expanding frontiers, religion and morals declined all over the colonies. In fact, even the churches were filled with unconverted. To meet such a need came the Great Awakening. The Awakening began with Theodore Frelinghuysen's preaching among the Dutch Reformed of New Jersey in the 1720s. Of Pietistic persuasion, Frelinghuysen apparently began his revivalistic efforts soon after he came over from Holland in 1720. By 1726, revival fires were burning not only among the Dutch Reformed of the Raritan River valley, but also among the Presbyterians of the area. Frelinghuysen especially influenced the Presbyterian pastors William and Gilbert Tennent, who worked among the Scotch-Irish in New Jersey.

Next the revival spread to the Congregationalists through the preaching of Jonathan Edwards, though there is no evidence that he had any communication with Frelinghuysen or that he was influenced by revival in the Middle Colonies. Under Edwards's preaching a revival broke out in his parish at Northampton, Massachusetts, in 1734. According to his statement, some three hundred of the town's eleven hundred people were converted in about six months. From Edwards's parish at the head of the Connecticut River valley, other revival fires spread down the valley and helped prepare the way for George Whitefield's ministry.

Whitefield, associate of the Wesleys, began his first great American tour in 1739 and preached with tremendous success during that year and the following in New England and the Middle Colonies. Because frequently there were no buldings large enough to hold the crowds, he preached in the open. Subsequently a great revival swept the region in 1741 and 1742. The Awakening spread to Presbyterians in Virginia through the work of Samuel Morris and Samuel Davies after 1740, and to the Baptists of North Carolina in 1755 through the work of Shubal Stearns and his brother-in-law Daniel Marshall. The Baptists had great success in Virginia, too. On the eve of the Revolution, a revival broke out in the South under the leadership of the Methodists, especially through the work of John King, Robert Williams, and Francis Asbury. Though Whitefield put much stress on emotionalism and incurred considerable opposition during his 1739-1740 tour, he changed his approach when he returned in 1744. Though results were proportionately smaller in New England on that occasion, in Pennsylvania, Maryland, and the South his efforts were tremendously successful. As may be seen from the dates given above, the Great Awakening in its various phases continued from the 1720s to the beginning of the Revolution.

Its results were phenomenal. Careful study of the church records of New England will show that earlier estimates that at least 10 percent of the population of the area was converted in the Awakening are probably correct. Thousands were swept into the Kingdom in the Middle and Southern Colonies. Baptists in Virginia alone reaped a harvest of some ten thousand souls between 1759 and 1776. Second, there was a quickening along missionary and educational lines. David Brainerd, Jonathan Edwards, and others preached to the Indians, and some effort was made to reach blacks with the gospel. Among the colleges to rise from the Awakening were Princeton (Presbyterian), Rutgers (Dutch Reformed), Brown (Baptist), and Dartmouth (Congregational). Dartmouth was founded as a training school to prepare Indians to serve as missionaries to their own people. Third, the revival contributed to the rise of religious liberty because it greatly increased the number of persons outside the established churches.

Fourth, it proved to be divisive in that among the Congregationalists and Presbyterians especially arose groups for and
against the revival. Later many of the Congregationalists opposed
to it slipped into the Unitarian camp. Fifth, the Awakening
brought to prominence Jonathan Edwards, who has been called
"America's greatest theologian" and "America's only original
theologian." Last, the revival preserved the American religious
heritage and assured its perpetuity amid the desolation of the
Revolution. And it may be argued that it prepared many individuals for the stresses and strains of the Revolutionary period.

RELIGIOUS DECLINE

The Revolutionary War was hard on religious life in America.
Because the churches so generally supported the Revolution, the
British took out their spite on houses of worship. Moreover,
many churches were destroyed when they were used for bar-
racks, hospitals, and storage of military equipment. Pastors and
their people were absorbed in the cause of the Revolution rather
than in building up the churches, and French deism and atheism
were fashionable because of alliance with France. In fact, rationalism took control in the colleges and other intellectual centers
of the land. In some colleges, there was hardly a student who
would admit to being a Christian. Conditions were so bad during
the years when the Constitution was being written and the new
nation was being launched that politicians and ministers alike
virtually gave up hope. For example, Bishop Samuel Provoost of
the Anglican Diocese of New York believed the situation so hope-
less that he simply ceased to function. A committee of Congress
reported on the desperate state of lawlessness on the frontier. Of
a population of five million, the United States had three hundred
thousand drunkards and buried about fifteen thousand of them
annually.[1] In 1796 George Washington agreed with a friend that
national affairs were leading to a crisis and he could not predict
what might happen.[2] Dark indeed were the closing years of the
eighteenth century. It is strange how distorted a view one gets

1. J. Edwin Orr, *The Eager Feet* (Chicago: Moody 1975), 8.
2. Ibid., 7.

from well-meaning preachers and patriots of the present who paint a rosy picture of conditions at the founding of the nation. There is little good that can be said of those times except that God was not through with the United States.

The Nineteenth Century

REVIVAL MOVEMENTS

Help was on the way. A few local revivals broke out in the early 1790s, but nothing extensive came until after the Concert of Prayer was launched. The eminent Massachusetts Baptist Isaac Backus and a score of other ministers called for the churches to engage in the Concert of Prayer for spiritual awakening, beginning on the first Tuesday in January, 1795, and continuing once a quarter thereafter. Denomination after denomination took up the challenge. Revivals began to break out everywhere around the turn of the century. The Second Evangelical Awakening was in progress (not only in America, but in Britain, on the Continent, and elsewhere). Revival fires burned over the entire nation, first in the East (especially Connecticut and Massachusetts) and then on the frontier. The revival was not characterized by evangelists going to and fro to incite churches to activity. There were few great names connected with it. For the most part, services were carried on by the pastors in their respective churches.

In New England the revival was quiet, not accompanied by emotional manifestations as during the Great Awakening. The situation on the frontier was different, however. There the Presbyterians inaugurated the camp meeting, to which thousands came from far and near. Emotional outbreaks were common in these meetings, but they have been greatly misrepresented or overplayed; and they did not seem to hinder the effect of the revival. Presbyterians, Methodists, and Baptists all worked side by side in these great gatherings, and all three benefited tremendously from the effort. One of the greatest of these camp meetings took place at Cane Ridge, Kentucky, in 1801, where it is said twenty-five thousand gathered in August. As many as five preachers addressed the crowds simultaneously in different places on the grounds. As elsewhere, Presbyterians, Methodists, and Baptists cooperated in the venture. Reportedly the character of Kentucky and Tennessee was completely changed by these meetings.

The effects of the Second Evangelical Awakening were tremendous: (1) The colleges of the land were largely reclaimed through the overthrow of infidelity. (2) There was a spiritual quickening in nearly all denominations, with tens of thousands being added to the Baptists, the Methodists, and the Presbyterians. (3) Lines were more clearly drawn between rationalism and evangelicalism, and there was a split between the Unitarians and evangelicals in the Congregational church. (4) The midweek prayer meeting and Sunday schools became common features of church life. (5) Close to a score of new colleges and seminaries were founded. (6) Missionary endeavor was spurred. The American Board of Commissioners for Foreign Missions came into being in 1810; one of its first missionaries was Adoniram Judson. The American Bible Society was founded in 1816, the American Tract Society in 1825.

As the Second Evangelical Awakening began to lose some of its force, Charles G. Finney came on the scene with his revival efforts. Beginning in New York State in 1824, he conducted very effective meetings in several Eastern cities. The greatest took place in Rochester, New York, in the fall and winter of 1830-1831, when he reported one thousand conversions. At the same time there were about one hundred thousand conversions in other parts of the country from New England to the Southwest. In 1835 Finney became president of Oberlin College in Ohio, where he continued to be an influential revivalist through personal campaigns and the wide distribution of his *Lectures on Revival.* The teachings of Finney and his associates Asa Mahan and Thomas Upham included entire consecration, sinless perfection in this life, and freedom of the will. Finney is given credit for introducing the anxious bench (the place to which inquirers went forward for conversion) and the cottage prayer meeting (at which non-Christians were prayed for by name in meetings in private homes). Out of the Oberlin School came the Holiness and Pentecostal churches. Not only did Finney's work make a great impact on America, but he also made two trips to Europe, where he experienced extensive success.

Another great revival spread across the country in 1858-1859. It was quite different from other revivals in that it not only did not have a series of great names attached to it, but those most responsible for its success were laymen. Moreover, it was enthusiastically supported by almost all Protestant denominations and was reported favorably by the press—which helped to make it the success it was. The usual view is that this revival began among the business people of New York and that the bank panic had something to do with scaring people into a new dependence on God. J. Edwin Orr, in communication with the writer, presents evidence to show that this view is erroneous. The revival began in Canada in September of 1857, and the first outbreaks in the United States occurred in Virginia and the Carolinas among slaves, who did not have any money at all. Ultimately over one hundred thousand blacks were converted in the 1858 revival.

But it is true that the movement gained momentum through the efforts of Jeremiah Lanphier, a city missionary in New York, who distributed handbills calling for weekly noon prayer meetings at the North Dutch Church beginning September 23, 1857. People were invited to come for five or ten minutes or to stay the whole hour if they could. Soon it became necessary to schedule daily meetings at other churches, halls, and theaters; and the movement spread to Philadelphia, Albany, Boston, Chicago, and other cities North and South. It is estimated that there were at least one million conversions in the United States during 1858 and 1859, with proportionately as great a revival in the South as the North, in spite of the slavery agitation of the period. In 1859 the influence of the revival spread to the British Isles, where it is said that another million made professions of faith. The awakening also touched many European countries, South Africa, India, the East and West Indies, and Canada. The revival continued after the War Between the States and in its later stages was even more visible in the South than the North. During the war, in 1861, a revival broke out among Confederate forces around Richmond and became a general moving of the Spirit by 1863. Though estimates vary, probably fifty thousand or more were converted in this awakening among the troops. Higher figures given in some accounts of this revival seem to be too generous.

One of the greatest modern revivalists was D. L. Moody, whose preaching was of the old evangelical type: a middle-of-the-road Calvinism rather than the Arminian approach of Finney and the Holiness preaching of the century. He urged predominantly the love of God as the great reason for repentance. Starting out in the YMCA and army camps during the Civil War, he conducted mass evangelism campaigns with the assistance of Ira D. Sankey in the large cities during the last three decades of the century. Not only did he have remarkable success in this country, but he made several trips to England. One of the most notable of these was the 1873-1875 campaign, during which he preached to more than 2.5 million people in London alone. Before the London crusade, he had conducted successful evangelistic efforts in other major cities of England and Scotland. One of his better-known accomplishments was the founding of the Moody Bible Institute. R. A. Torrey, J. Wilbur Chapman, and other evangelists followed. And revivalism has been a continuing characteristic of American Christianity.

Not the least of the later revivals in the United States was the awakening of 1905. Part of a worldwide movement and apparently especially inspired by British revivals, it touched all parts of the country and made its impact in Canada as well. Northern Methodists reported an increase of over 200,000 in 1905-1906; Lutherans, 167,000; Baptists, 165,000; and Presbyterians, 67,000. Revivals hit college campuses in several parts of the country. Missionary effort was greatly stimulated. The complete story may be found in J. Edwin Orr's *The Flaming Tongue.*

THE SLAVERY ISSUE

Revivalism was one very important feature of American Christianity in the nineteenth century; a second was agitation over the slavery issue and dissolution of the union. Widespread antislavery sentiment found expression in the formation of numerous antislavery societies in the latter years of the eighteenth century and the early years of the nineteenth century. After the formation in 1816 of The American Society for the Colonization of the Free People of Color in the United States, interest settled especially on relocation of blacks in Liberia, and anti-slavery agitation virtually came to an end.

Then, about 1830, a new phase of the anti-slavery movement began. By that time the full effects of Eli Whitney's cotton gin were being felt, and the demand for cotton fastened the plantation system ever more firmly on the South. Southern leaders found support for the institution of slavery in the Bible, "both by precept and example." Meanwhile aggressive anti-slavery propagandists such as William Lloyd Garrison (editor of the *Liberator*), Wendell Phillips, and Theodore Parker arose in the North, especially in New England. Those radical Boston Unitarians were joined by people such as Harriet Beecher Stowe, Finney's convert Theodore Dwight Weld, the Presbyterian brothers Arthur and Lewis Tappan, and the Quaker sisters Sarah and Angeline Grimké, all from evangelical backgrounds. Soon antislavery societies sprang up in the churches, and some religious bodies began to pass strong antislavery resolutions. In 1833, the American Anti-Slavery Society was organized, and Arthur Tappan was its first president.

But the cause of abolitionism had its problems. In their zeal to emancipate the slaves, the radicals increasingly attacked the Constitution and the Bible, which were often used as supports for the "peculiar institution." Evangelicals, as Bible believers and loyal Americans, could not condone the blanket attacks being hurled against the government and Christianity. By 1845 Garrison had ousted all evangelicals from the American Anti-Slavery Society. Evangelicals also had problems within their ranks. A great many of them had come to believe that the churches of America had a mission to Christianize the nation and the world. If the issue of slavery were allowed to fracture the churches and the nation, then all was lost. So, many leaders wanted to silence abolitionist sentiment and work out compromises that would at all costs preserve the unity of the church and the unity of the nation. Perhaps this attitude concerning America's place in world missions and the union of the nation helps to explain why almost every major religious body in the North gave such generous support to the Federal government during the war. In fact, maintenance of the unity of church and the unity of the nation became more precious than abolition of slavery.

In spite of efforts at compromise and conciliation, ruptures along sectional lines took place in one after another of the major religious bodies. The rank and file of American church members in the North did not feel that they had to choose between abolition on the one hand and Christianity and patriotism on the other. They did not buy the whole of Garrison's argument, and Charles Finney in his role of a winner of souls possibly won as many to the cause of abolition as did Garrison. Of course other religious leaders made their contributions to the rise of abolitionist sentiment. The gulf widened between Northern and Southern church members. In 1843 the Wesleyan Methodist Connection organized in Utica, New York. Two years later the Methodist Episcopal Church, South, organized in Louisville, Kentucky. In the same month (May 1845), the Southern Baptist Convention was founded in Augusta, Georgia. New School Presbyterians[3] divided in 1858, Old School Presbyterians in 1861, and the Lutherans in 1863. The period following the war marked the efforts of the churches to unite once more.

SOCIAL CONCERNS

Out of the same context as evangelical concern for the plight of the blacks came an interest in alleviating many other ills of society. The perfectionist, or sanctification, preaching of Charles Finney, Asa Mahan, Walter and Phoebe Palmer, William and Catherine Booth, and many others, especially in the Methodist and Holiness camps, promoted concern for eradication not only of personal sin, but also of the sins of society. They believed that only the power of the Spirit of God ultimately could solve the ills of society and that personal holiness led one to be a servant of his fellow men. The social concerns of many evangelicals coincided with those of such liberal leaders as Washington Gladden and

3. The Presbyterian church underwent a schism in 1837, and the New School formed its own organization the following year. The New School (composing 4/9 of the church) was the more liberal element in doctrine and in organizational approach. After the Old and New Schools had split along sectional lines, the two southern groups united as the Presbyterian Church in the Confederate States (later Presbyterian Church in the United States) in 1864.

Walter Rauschenbusch, who wanted to deal with a host of problems plaguing society during the nineteenth century. But in this movement the preponderance of numbers and wealth lay on the side of the evangelicals.

One of the first social problems to receive attention was alcoholism. In 1836 two nationwide organizations merged to form the American Temperance Union, designed to urge moderation. In 1840 the Washington Temperance Society was founded to encourage total abstinence. The aim of the movement was not to control private behavior, but to reform society; drunkenness was viewed as the prime cause of pauperism. State prohibition was first enacted in Maine in 1851.

Various evangelical agencies developed a new concern for those whom the industrial system had relegated to the city slums. Such organizations as the American Sunday School Union and the Home Missionary and Tract societies moved from simple evangelism to the establishment of Sunday schools and mission churches, job placement, distribution of food and clothing to the poor, and resettlement of destitute youth. Phoebe Palmer did important pioneer work in social welfare projects in New York, engaging in prison ministry at the Tombs, participating in the work of The New York Female Assistance Society for the Relief and Religious Instruction of the Sick Poor, supporting an orphanage, and founding in 1850 the Five Points Mission. The latter marked the beginning of Protestant institutional work in the slums. In conjunction with this settlement house, Morris Pease established the Five Points House of Industry, which by 1854 supported five hundred people. Mrs. Palmer also helped to organize in 1858 the Ladies Christian Association of New York, which pioneered in programs that the YWCA was later to carry on. About the same time, others founded a home for the deaf and a shelter for black orphans in New York. Missions to immigrants and sailors were established in New York, Boston, and other cities. William E. Boardman served as executive secretary during some of the most effective years of the United States Christian Commission, organized in New York in 1861 to meet both spiritual and physical needs of servicemen.

During and after the Civil War the churches became more alert to their social obligations. City rescue missions, orphanages, hospitals, homes for the aged, and other agencies were established to meet the needs of various groups. The YMCA and YWCA movements spread rapidly across the country to meet city youths' need for lodging, social activity, and Bible study. At the end of the war, in 1866, the several church-sponsored freedmen's relief associations united as the American Freedmen's Union Commission to aid freed slaves. One could go on and on with names of organizations and individuals, but these examples will suffice. Some of the most effective and best-known efforts took place in New York, Philadelphia, and Boston, but the churches rallied to aid the needy in many centers of the land.

RISE OF LIBERALISM

As noted above, by no means all those engaged in social action were evangelicals. And even some of the evangelicals in time neglected their biblical underpinnings, continuing to feed the hungry but forgetting to do it in the name of Christ. The name most commonly associated with the rise of the Social Gospel is Walter Rauschenbusch (1861-1918). Pastor of a Baptist church in New York (beginning in 1886), where he came to know human need firsthand, he later joined the faculty of Colgate-Rochester Theological Seminary, where he wrote influential books: *Christianity and the Social Crisis* (1907), *Christianizing the Social Order* (1912), and *A Theology for the Social Gospel* (1917). Though he started out early in life with a belief in original sin and personal salvation, by the time he got to his last book he viewed sin as social and impersonal and taught that social reform would come with the demise of capitalism, the advance of socialism, and the establishment of the kingdom of God. Rauschenbusch's views found ready acceptance by such spokesmen as Shailer Matthews and Shirley Jackson Case, both at the University of Chicago.

The impact of Rauschenbusch must be added to other threads in the development of liberalism during the nineteenth century. At the beginning of the century Unitarianism made deep inroads under the leadership of such outstanding spokesmen as William

Ellery Channing (1780-1842) and Theodore Parker (1810-1860). Channing's sermon "Unitarian Christianity" (1819) receives credit for launching the Unitarian controversy.

Another influential figure of the century was Horace Bushnell (1802-1876). Bushnell published his *Christian Nurture* in 1847 and argued that a child should grow up in a Christian home as a child of the covenant, never knowing he was anything but a Christian. His idea of growth into grace made a profound impact on generations of Christian educators and muted the requirement of a conversion experience in the preaching and teaching of numerous church groups.

In addition to his support of Unitarianism, Theodore Parker also did much to introduce German biblical criticism into American Christianity. Thus the way was prepared for the impact of Darwinian evolution and the ideas of Julius Wellhausen (see chap. 7). Wellhausen's views, especially as interpreted by such English scholars as S. R. Driver, drew an exceptionally large following. A theological liberalism grew up, based on the twin postulates of the evolution of religion and the denial of the supernatural, and teaching such concepts as the fatherhood of God and brotherhood of man and the institution of the kingdom of God as an evolutionary outcome of the effort of churchmen in society.

Also important to American liberal development during the nineteenth century was the work of three German scholars: Schleiermacher, Ritschl, and Harnack. Friedrich Schleiermacher (1768-1834) made experience or feeling the basis of the faith, rather than the Bible and one's relationship to Christ. Religion involved a feeling of absolute dependence on God. Doctrine was for him contingent on religious experience, not experience on revealed doctrine. Jesus showed the way of absolute dependence on God and of love to man.

Albert Ritschl (1822-1889) taught, among other things, that Christ's death had nothing to do with payment of a penalty for sin, but resulted from loyalty to His calling. It was His objective to establish the kingdom of God. He would share with men His consciousness of sonship and help them to realize God's goal of living together in mutual love. The practice of religion in com-

munity was of vital importance because Christ could best communicate Himself to men through the community He had founded (the church). Ritschl's strong social emphasis contributed to
the Social Gospel of the time, and his impact on numerous scholars was great.

Especially was Adolf Harnack (1851-1930) a follower of
Ritschl. Like Ritschl, he saw Pauline Hellenism as an intrusion
on early Christian thought and chose to emphasize the ethical
aspects of Christianity. While professor at Berlin in 1901 he published his influential *What Is Christianity?* This focused on the
human qualities of Christ, who preached not about Himself but
about the Father; the kingdom and the fatherhood of God; a
higher righteousness; and the command to love. The views of
these men soon washed ashore in America and helped to further
the ideas of the fatherhood of God and brotherhood of man and
the gradual establishment of the kingdom of God in cooperation
with the Deity.

The churches did not take lightly the liberal attacks on conservative theology. Charles A. Briggs, professor at Union Theological
Seminary in New York, was put on trial before the Presbytery of
New York and suspended from the ministry in 1893. Henry P.
Smith of Lane Seminary in Cincinnati was likewise defrocked by
the Presbyterian church in 1893. In the same year A. C. McGiffert
was dismissed from Lane for his liberal views. Other denominations also had heresy trials and dismissed or disciplined offend-
ing persons. Probably the most famous conflict of the twentieth
century concerned Harry Emerson Fosdick, who in 1925 was
forced out of the pastorate of First Presbyterian Church of New
York City and became an influential spokesman for liberalism
from the pulpit of the Riverside Church until his retirement in
1946.

Roman Catholicism likewise suffered the inroads of liberalism
and reacted strongly against it. Alfred Loisy, founder of Roman
Catholic modernism in France, was dismissed in 1893 from his
professorship at the Institut Catholique in Paris and excommunicated in 1908. The English Jesuit George Tyrrell was demoted in
1899 and died out of fellowship with the church. Liberalism also
invaded American Roman Catholicism. To silence the threat

worldwide, Pope Pius X issued the decree *Lamentabili* in 1907, and in 1910 he imposed an antimodernist oath on the clergy.

In contesting with rising liberalism, evangelicalism had a number of able scholars during the latter part of the nineteenth century and the early part of the twentieth. Charles Hodge defended a supernaturally inspired Bible during his long tenure as professor of biblical literature and later of theology at Princeton Seminary (1820-1878). A. A. Hodge ably succeeded his father at Princeton (1877-1886). In 1887 B. B. Warfield followed Hodge as professor of theology at Princeton. At home in Hebrew, Greek, modern languages, theology, and biblical criticism, he staunchly defended an inerrant Scripture and cardinal evangelical doctrines in a score of books and numerous pamphlets. In 1900 the scholarly Robert Dick Wilson joined the Princeton faculty, and J. Gresham Machen came to the faculty in 1906. In 1929, when a liberal realignment occurred at Princeton, Machen and Wilson joined Oswald T. Allis, Cornelius Van Til, and others in founding Westminster Theological Seminary. Of course other scholars could be mentioned, but these were some of the most vocal and the most prestigious.

While some evangelical scholars were standing for the faith in academic circles, a large number of faith missions came into existence to propagate the gospel on foreign fields. A few of them include: Africa Inland Mission, 1895; Central American Mission, 1890; Scandinavian Alliance Mission (now The Evangelical Alliance Mission), 1890; The Regions Beyond Missionary Union, 1878; Sudan Interior Mission, 1893.

Meanwhile, other groups that differed to a greater or lesser degree from mainline positions appeared on the American religious scene. The Mormon movement came into being in 1830, the Seventh-Day Adventists[4] the following year, Spiritualism in 1848, Russellism (or Jehovah's Witnesses) in 1872, and Christian Science in 1876.

---

4. Seventh-Day Adventists are now operating in 185 countries with a total membership of 3,750,000. Membership in the United States stands at 571,000. Comments on Mormons and Jehovah's Witnesses appear in the next chapter. The Christian Science movement does not publish membership figures, but it is known to have declined in popularity in recent years.

American Christianity has been characterized by full religious freedom, the separation of church and state, the voluntary principle of church membership, a democratic approach both in government and in lay participation, a high degree of informality in worship services, and a tendency toward the multiplication of denominations and sects.

9

The Present Situation

How do we stand some two thousand years after Christ delivered the Great Commission?[1] Christianity is still a minority faith. This is true whether one accepts the figure of a billion and a half Christians in the world as of mid-1985 (as posited in the *World Christian Encyclopedia*) or the lesser number of a billion (1982 *Encyclopedia Britannica Book of the Year*). In any case it appears that the percentage of Christians in the world today is less than it was at its peak of about 34 percent in 1900. Although Christianity has been making tremendous advances in Africa, Latin America, and elsewhere, these are more than offset by the effects of materialism in Europe and America, the impediment of atheistic Communism behind the Iron and Bamboo Curtains, and the high

---

1. The account presented in this chapter is based on endless contacts with church leaders all over the United States and in England, where leaders from the Continent were interviewed. Many of the statistics and other details about various ministries (e.g., Campus Crusade, Inter-Varsity, Jews for Jesus, and Bible distribution organizations) were obtained in oral and written statements made directly to the writer by the directors or other officers or statisticians of the organizations discussed. The writer expresses his appreciation for the kind responses to many telephone calls to organizational headquarters. Denominational membership statistics, attendance records, and other pertinent facts are published annually in the *Yearbook of American and Canadian Churches, The World Almanac,* and in less detail in the *Encyclopedia Britannica Book of the Year.*

birth rate in the Muslim world and in India.[2] In spite of the slight decline in the percentage of Christians worldwide, they make up more than half of the population in two-thirds of the world's 223 countries.

Not only is Christianity still a minority faith, it is also still under assault. Such a condition is to be expected, because Jesus never promised that His followers would win the world with the preaching of the gospel or would establish a utopia. Only the return of Christ in person will achieve that. Moreover, He never promised that His church would be immune from attack: "the world . . . hated Me; . . . therefore the world hates you" (John 15:18-19). Though opposition to Christianity will certainly come in all periods of history, it assumes new forms in each age. External forces contending with the church have been at least fourfold in recent decades: Communism, nationalism and national or pagan religion, cults, and social assault.

External Opposition to Christianity

Karl Marx formulated his economic, political, and religious philosophy about the middle of the last century as an antidote to a rampant capitalism. He appealed to the downtrodden workers in industrial nations to throw off the bondage with which they were yoked and to introduce a new classless society. But in industrial nations the lot of the worker slowly improved through the efforts of labor unions and reformers and through governmental intervention. So, it was in the great agrarian nation of Russia, unresponsive to change and the needs of the masses, that Communism, as reconstructed or reinterpreted by Lenin, first caught fire. Now it has engulfed some 1.6 billion people out of a total world population of 4.7 billion and knocks at the door of many countries in Asia, the Middle East, Latin America, Africa, and Europe.

Wherever it has gone, this atheistic system has sought utterly to uproot Christianity—either by direct onslaught or by subver-

2. The total population of the earth is now set at over 4.7 billion. The Muslim population has risen to about 900 million and the Hindu population to about 580 million. "Christian" as used in this chapter refers to all varieties of Christians, unless it is specifically used in a more restrictive sense.

sion. Although Communism has not been able to obliterate Christianity in the countries where it has won control, it has surely proved to be a formidable enemy. In Russia and China and some other countries, official churches of sorts have been permitted, both to provide some impression to the world of freedom of religion and to control more effectively religious expression. The true church is largely underground in all Communist countries. Bible printing and importing are now allowed in East Germany, Poland, and Yugoslavia, and minimally in Russia and China, but in most other Communist countries Bibles are difficult to virtually impossible to get. The scarcity of Scripture is most critical in Bulgaria, Albania, Russia, and China.

Opposition to or persecution of Christianity in most Marxist-dominated states is covert. Christians are prohibited from attendance at university and from advancement into prestigious positions. Sometimes they are even fired from menial employment. Efforts are made to choke off a supply of trained leadership of churches by severely restricting the numbers permitted to matriculate in theological seminaries. In order to prevent adequate places for meeting, building permits often are denied to churches or tied up in bureaucratic red tape for long periods of time. Pastors may be intimidated, as was true in the fall of 1982 in Romania when four leading Baptist pastors were accused of embezzling church funds for affirming separation of church and state and for opposition to state interference in church affairs.

In recent years Russian KGB agents have posed as Bible smugglers to ferret out Christians. It is also common in Russia for Christians to be accused of having mental illness and to be assigned to mental hospitals for "treatment." In Czechoslovakia, during the last couple of years secret agents have been specially trained to comb the mountainous Slovakian countryside to detect prayer meetings, Bible studies, and discussion groups. It is hard to discover how many believers may be in prison for their faith at any one time in a given country, but the research center at Keston College in England reported that there were 307 known Christian prisoners in the Soviet Union at the beginning of 1981. Strong evidence indicates that Christians and other dissidents provided some of the slave labor that built the gas pipeline from Siberia to Western Europe.

Of course not all the opposition is covert or indirect. As a case in point, in Marxist Ethiopia late in 1982 authorities in Wollega Province closed 284 of the 350 churches of the Lutheran Ethiopian Evangelical church there. And as is well known, the Cultural Revolution in China (1965-1968) openly made war on Christianity and tried by every means to destroy it.

Nationalism and national religions also vie with Christianity for mastery. Where nationalistic movements have resulted in the creation of new states, the religious body with the largest number of adherents has tended to assume leadership and establish a state religion. For example, Muslims predominate in Pakistan and Indonesia, Hindus in India, and Buddhists in Burma. Therefore Christian work does not enjoy the freedom that existed under friendly British or Dutch governments. Moreover, in many countries Christianity has been linked in the minds of the people with Western imperialism. Now that those countries have cut the cord that binds them to a foreign power, they find it more difficult to accept the religion of that power. And strongly nationalistic peoples do not care to be evangelized from abroad; such activity puts them on an inferior level.

The impact of nationalism or new national conditions on Christianity is evident from such examples as the following. In 1973 the Somali Republic nationalized all mission programs and facilities; Singapore nationalized all private schools; the Pakistani government took over the Protestant and Roman Catholic colleges of the country; and President Amin of Uganda expelled fifty-eight European missionaries and ordered Africanization of the country's churches. In 1975 the government of Mozambique proclaimed religion to be a divisive force and confiscated all missionary funds and property; President Tombalbaye of Chad severely persecuted Christians in a continuing effort to return the country to its traditional animism (but his assassination stopped the persecution); President Ngeuma of Equatorial Guinea campaigned against all believers in God and turned many churches into warehouses; and President Mobutu Sese Seko of Zaire continued his moves against Christianity by forbidding religious instruction in the country's school system, 90 percent of which was operated by religious organizations. In 1980, evangelical radio programs were totally banned in Mexico; and recently Bibles placed in Israeli hotels by the Gideons were removed and destroyed.

By no means do all these nationalistic movements augur ill for true Christianity. For instance, although nearly all foreign missionaries were expelled from Burma in 1966, Christianity is healthy and growing there. Revival broke out in the Kachin tribal area of northern Burma in 1980. As a result Baptists there now number 90,000, and members of the Assemblies of God number 50,000. In 1972, after three Indian states had passed laws declaring conversion to Christianity illegal, Prime Minister Indira Gandhi and the Indian Parliament declared those laws null and void. Hostility to Christianity in Nepal has not prevented some expansion there either. In 1975 there were only 500 baptized Christians in the country when Adon Rongong returned home from some Christian training in the Philippines. As he challenged other believers to greater evangelization, they began to witness for Christ. By 1979 the number of baptized believers had grown to 8,000; and by 1982 the number had increased to 20,000 in a population of about 15 million. Moreover, the support of governments for Roman Catholic persecution of Protestants in Spain and Latin America has largely ceased.

A third threat to true Christianity is the cults and Eastern philosophies and religions. However, it may be said that the cults tend to breed where Christianity has failed; untaught or disenchanted adherents of Christianity rather than the completely unchurched constitute the most fertile ground in which cultists may plant their seed. In the United States at least, Russellism (Jehovah's Witnesses) spreads most rapidly among the unsophisticated. Mormonism has gained especially in the Northwest, but has been successful among all classes in various parts of the country and abroad. There are now more than 2.4 million Jehovah's Witnesses worldwide, including 565 thousand in the United States. The Mormons (Church of Jesus Christ of Latter-day Saints) have been extremely successful in winning converts. Beginning the century with 250 thousand followers, they increased to 1 million by 1950, doubled to 2 million by 1964, and more than doubled again to reach 5 million in 1982. They claim 2,965,000 members in the various branches in the United States and have become the dominant religious group in 74 counties in Utah, Idaho, and adjacent states. This is more than twice the number of counties as had a majority of Mormon churches in 1971. They have about 100,000 members in Britain and 30,000 missionaries in 83 countries. They organized dioceses in Italy and Portugal in 1981 and in Spain in 1982. Other groups do not demonstrate the same degree of aggressive evangelism as the Jehovah's Witnesses and Mormons and thus do not so greatly threaten orthodox Christianity.

It is not quite so easy to quantify the impact of Eastern religions in the West in general, or in the United States in particular. Transcendental meditation makes its influence felt broadly in American society. The *Tao Te Ching*, the sacred book of Taoism, often may be purchased at the corner bookstore. Writings of the Hare Krishna movement, which comes from the context of Hinduism, often may be picked up at an airport, especially in Los Angeles, New York, or London. There are more than 3 million Muslims and 250 thousand Buddhists in the United States; this includes 2 million Black Muslims, a movement that is growing rapidly. Members of the Baha'i faith support their magnificent temple in Wilmette, Illinois, which dwarfs the temple at the international headquarters of the religion.

A fourth threat to the church is the social assault. Television with its constant discrediting of Christianity and its moral standards, pornography and the increase of sexual looseness, the rise in the divorce rate, the plague of the drug traffic, and the alcoholic craze are only some of the better-known aspects of society that bombard the church, the Christian family, and the individual. The constancy and the intensity of the attack periodically cause the weaker to fall. The environment of the Christian is increasingly polluted. For instance, a Gallup Poll conducted in 1981 reported that one in four claimed that an alcohol-related problem affected his family life; this was up from one in eight in 1974. Alcohol abuse was cited by one in four as one of the three reasons most responsible for the high divorce rate in the United States. A survey released in 1983 concluded that of high school seniors in the United States about one-third get drunk once a month and about one-fourth get high on marijuana once a month. Christians will find it hard to stand against the current. But there is the same power in the gospel today as there was during the first century. It was to Christians living in a completely pagan society that Paul wrote, "Do not be conformed [pressed into the mold] to this world" (Romans 12:2).

Developments Within Christianity

ECUMENICAL EFFORTS

So much for the external forces that Christianity has to meet today. Now it remains to look at what has been going on within the ranks. Throughout the century there has been great interest in ecumenical or union movements. Part of this effort seemingly has come about because some people honestly felt that the church was too fragmented and that it ought to present a more united front to the world. And part of it seemed to result from the loss of doctrinal distinctives that tended to keep groups separate. The ecumenical spirit especially expressed itself in the United States in the work of the Federal Council of the Churches of Christ in America, organized in 1908. This body reorganized in 1950 as the National Council of Churches of Christ in America and became a much more comprehensive organization. The Council's member churches now have an aggregate membership of approximately 40 million. Some right-wing conservatives organized the American Council of Churches in 1941 as their answer to the generally liberal-minded National Council, but subsequently this group fragmented and became less effective. More in the mainstream of American evangelicalism is the National Association of Evangelicals, organized in 1942 as a means of bringing together conservative Protestant churches. This body now has 3.5 million members.

Then in 1948, after many years of preparation,[3] the World

3. The Edinburgh Missionary Conference of 1910 led some to think of a united Church, and in that year Faith and Order was organized. This society concerned itself with differences in belief among the churches. Subsequently the Life and Work Movement was founded to deal with social and political responsibilities of the churches. These organizations were involved with conferences at Lausanne in 1927 and Edinburgh in 1937; at the latter a decision was reached to form a World Council of Churches. A provisional constitution was drawn up at Utrecht in 1938, but the war prevented formal organization until the Amsterdam meeting in 1948.

Council of Churches was formed at Amsterdam, with 147 denominations from forty-four countries participating. With the passage of time the Eastern Orthodox church (but not the Roman Catholic church) has joined the world body, but evangelicals generally have not become involved.

Both the National Council and the World Council have been criticized for being too theologically liberal and too politicized in favor of leftist causes. The National Council especially has been scored even in the secular press for its leftist leanings and its financial support for revolutionary or at least Marxist-oriented movements. Its employment of revolutionary slogans and rhetoric and its tendency to portray the United States in a bad light while it glosses over the faults of revolutionary movements and glorifies their achievements, have given the Council bad press and increasingly have put it on the defensive. Many have concluded that the church has become too political.

Those who have been worried about theological liberalism and political activity of the World Council of Churches took some consolation in the direction of the Sixth Assembly of the Council in Vancouver in 1983. After the Fifth Assembly at Uppsala in 1968 supported liberation theologies, sent money to liberation movements, and criticized failures of the West, many evangelicals believed the Council had drifted irretrievably to the left. At Vancouver, however, there was greatly increased attention to a vigorous Trinitarian theology and evangelistic proclamations, and there was a backdrop of prayer with round-the-clock prayer for the sessions throughout the assembly. A majority of evangelicals present drafted an open letter commending the evangelical concerns at the assembly and calling for evangelical involvement with the World Council of Churches. But a minority opinion saw the evangelical indications at the assembly to be only half the story. They reacted against the continuing theological vagueness, support for liberation theologies, and unbalanced criticism of the West, and urged evangelicals to avoid involvement with the World Council of Churches.

While the National and World Councils have been involved in social and political action in a more liberal theological context, the Moral Majority has sought to engage in social action in a conservative theological context. The Moral Majority was organized by Jerry Falwell, pastor of Thomas Road Baptist Church in Lynchburg, Virginia, in 1979. It has enlisted more than 4 million members, including 72,000 ministers. It hopes to organize the evangelical and fundamentalist Christians of the United States, as well as others holding to traditional moral values. The movement opposes permissiveness and moral relativism, wants to restore the sacredness of the family and human life, seeks to wage war against illegal drug traffic and pornography, and firmly supports a strong national defense and the state of Israel.

A certain amount of hope arose in some circles that all churches might eventually get together, as Roman Catholics launched an ecumenical council, Vatican II, in 1962. Observers who were not Roman Catholics were welcomed and "heretics" henceforth became "separated brethren." In fact, long before the first session of the council met, on May 30, 1960, Pope John XXIII had established a Secretariat for Church Unity to facilitate the reunion of separated brethren into the one fold of Christ. Some saw a connection between the calling of an ecumenical council and the ecumenical movement. Pope John did not simply invite all others to return to the fold of Rome; he called for a renewal of the Roman church so that it would be more credible to the separated brethren. The council was characterized by a new spirit of openness. This was demonstrated by the invitation to non-Roman Catholics to attend, by the unprecedented publicity given the event, and by the degree of flexibility and the irenic tone often expressed in dealing with non-Roman Catholics. A new missionary spirit and the responsibility of the church to serve in the world received emphasis.

The council met in four sessions—1962, 1963, 1964, 1965— under John XXIII and Paul VI (about twenty-five hundred delegates came from 136 countries, in addition to Orthodox and Protestant observers). Though Pope Paul was regarded as a liberal, he viewed with alarm the radical character of some of the proposals of the council and intervened to moderate them. But even so, considerable changes occurred, not in basic doctrine, but in approaches and attitudes. Pope John saw that the church had to prepare itself to serve a changed and changing world, and that modernization was necessary to make the church intelligible to modern man. The church had to recover its character as a living witness to God's love for man.

A total of sixteen constitutions or decrees came out of Vatican II.[4] Of special importance to the layman was permission to use vernacular languages in the liturgy; adaptation of rites to differing, non-Western cultures; and simplification of the liturgy. The "Constitution on Divine Revelation" changed the basis of authority in the church. Whereas the Council of Trent had in 1546 declared that Scripture and tradition were equal bases of authority, Vatican II did not distinguish between the two, but emphasized their interplay or interrelatedness. The place of the Bible in Romanism had been upgraded by a recent emphasis on biblical studies and the encouragement of Pius XII (1943) to follow literal interpretation of Scripture whenever possible. Now a conciliar decision tends to give greater official support to what has been happening in the church.

In the spirit of greater sharing of authority in the church, the council declared that infallibility of the church resides in the pope and also "in the body of bishops when that body exercises supreme teaching authority with the successor of Peter." Moreover, the "Constitution on the Church" stated: "Together with its head, the Roman pontiff, and never without its head, the episcopal order is the subject of the supreme and full power over the universal Church."

Of more importance to the world at large were the decisions on ecumenism. The "Constitution on the Church," as would be expected, defined the church as the people of God who were properly in the Roman communion. But it also included the baptized who "do not profess the faith in its entirety or do not preserve unity of communion with the successor of Peter." The decree on ecumenism, *Unitatis Redintegratio,* declared that both Roman Catholics and Protestants must share the blame for the division among Christians, called on Roman Catholics to play their part in the ecumenical movement, and set forth the importance of renewal as a prelude to unity. This was quite different

4. See A. P. Flannery, ed., *Documents of Vatican II* (Grand Rapids: Eerdmans, 1975).

from the old "return to the Fold" exhortation to Protestants. The "Decree on Eastern Catholic Churches," among other things, underscored the hope of the council for a corporate union of the Eastern churches not in union with the church at Rome. Near the close of the council, a prayer service took place at St. Paul's Outside the Walls, in which Pope Paul, the bishops of the council, and observers and guests joined in prayers for promoting Christian unity.

Twenty years after the calling of Vatican II the Roman Catholic church looks quite different from what it did before the Council. Now worship services are conducted in the language of the people. The priest often distributes both elements to participants in the communion and faces the congregation as he leads them in celebration of the sacrament. Biblical exposition and congregational singing are common elements of Catholic worship services. A Bible in the language of the people may at least be found in most American Catholic homes. Interaction between Catholics and Protestants has been much more pronounced as they have cooperated in social and political action, and as charismatics in both camps have enjoyed a common experience.

In addition to interdenominational cooperation, there has also been considerable organic union of churches in this century. The United Church of Canada came into being in 1925, the Church of South India in 1947, the National Church of Scotland in 1929, the Methodist Church in the United States in 1939, the United Church of Christ in 1961,[5] the Lutheran church and the Protestant Churches of Madagascar in 1982, the Presbyterian church in 1983, and a host of other unions have taken place at home and abroad. On September 8, 1982, the Lutheran Church in America, the American Lutheran Church, and the Association of Evangelical Lutheran Churches voted to merge to form a new church by 1988. The combined membership of these three bodies is just over 5,276,000. In September of 1982 a union of the Church of Christ in Madagascar and the Malagasy Lutheran Church oc-

5. The Congregational Church and the Christian Church merged in 1931, were joined by the Evangelical and Reformed Church in 1957, and completed their union with the adoption of a constitution for the United Church in 1961. Reported membership in 1982 was 1,726,000.

curred, with a membership of 1.5 million in a country of about 9 million. The Presbyterian Church is a union of the United Presbyterian Church in the U.S.A. and the Presbyterian Church in the U.S. (known as the Southern Presbyterians). The new church (which formally came into existence on June 10, 1983) has 3.2 million members, quite evenly distributed over the United States. The union ended 122 years of separation brought on by the Civil War. Roman Catholics and Anglicans are engaging in a dialogue preliminary to merger negotiations. Whether such questions as headship of the church and ordination of women can be settled to the satisfaction of both groups remains to be seen. Currently the 1.72 million member United Church of Christ and the 1.17 million member Christian Church (Disciples of Christ) are engaged in merger discussions, and a vote on the matter is being proposed.

INDICATIONS OF DECADENCE

In recent years it has become evident that all is not well within the churches. Worldwide the Roman Catholic church has found it increasingly difficult to control its constituency. Especially in Latin America and Europe, church attendance has been very low. For instance, in France, which is 85 percent Roman Catholic, attendance at mass is only 12 percent on a given Sunday, according to a recent survey; and a full one-third of French youth do not profess to believe in God. Closures of training schools for Catholic leadership have reached the point in some places in Europe that the church finds it increasingly difficult to supply needed personnel. Enrollment in Catholic seminaries in the United States has dropped from 47,500 to 12,000 in the last two decades. There is increasing opposition worldwide to the position of the hierarchy on birth control, divorce, and clerical celibacy.

Religion in Europe as a whole is in a decadent condition. As a leading European evangelical recently observed, "Europe is *the* mission field of the world." Only about 4 percent of the English were in church on a given Sunday as of about 1975. More than 500 Anglican churches were closed during the sixties and seventies. Defections from British Catholic churches are also exten-

sive. Britain has seemed almost to be in a process of de-chris-
tianization. The Church of Scotland lost nearly a quarter of its
membership during the sixteen years prior to 1983. Less than
one-fifth of Scots even nominally belong to the church. But Britain is much better off than the Lutheran countries. For example,
in Finland, though 92 percent of all adults had been baptized as
children by the Evangelical Lutheran Church, in 1980 only 3
percent of parishoners attended Sunday worship services. In
West Germany, the Evangelical Church (Lutheran) reported in
1980 that 42 percent of the population belonged to its churches,
but that only a little over 5 percent attended worship on Sundays.

But there are signs of spiritual life in Europe. In 1982 British
church attendance was up to about 11 percent of the adult population. One report estimates that fully one-third of all graduates
of Anglican seminaries now are evangelical. Luis Palau began his
"Mission to London" in October of 1983 and planned to extend
his crusade there to the summer of 1984; and at the same time
Billy Graham conducted crusades in the five other major English
cities of Liverpool, Bristol, Birmingham, Newcastle, and Nor-
wich. Expectancy of spiritual revitalization is in the air in England. Evangelicals in Sweden and Denmark are stirring and
advocating formation of their own segment of the state Lutheran
church. Some hints of new life were evident in Finland in 1980
and 1981. In 1982 Luis Palau conducted a crusade in Helsinki.
For the first time in 400 years state and free churches joined in
evangelism in a city where only about 1 percent attend church.
Over 1,400 responded to the invitation to accept Christ as Savior.
An estimated 3,500 to 5,000 groups of pietistic believers now
assemble in West Germany, some with memberships in the hundreds. Wuppertal is the center of this movement. About 600 such
groups may be found in the Wuppertal-Bonn area.

In the United States, though church membership has continued to grow during recent years it has not kept pace with the rate
of population increase. For example, it stood at about
131,400,000 in 1974; 132,812,000 in 1978; 133,388,000 in 1980,
and 134,817,000 in 1981. In 1973 church membership reached a
high of 62.4 percent of the population, but it has gradually declined since then. In 1974 it dipped to 61.9, in 1977 to 60.7, in

1980 to 60.5, and in 1981 to 58.7. Then in 1982 it jumped to 59.7 percent, with an increase of membership to 138,452,000. It is too early to tell whether the membership decline has been reversed or whether this one reporting year is merely an exception to the general trend. During 1982 there were about 76,350,000 Protestants, 51,207,000 Roman Catholics, 5,000,000 Eastern Orthodox, and 5,920,000 Jews in the United States.

A high point in church and synagogue attendance was reached in 1958 when 49 percent of adults attended in an average week. This figure has declined to only 40 percent in 1983. Roman Catholics suffered the greatest decline, from 74 percent in 1958 to 52 percent in 1978. They had a slight rebound to 53 percent in 1981. Protestants experienced a decline from 44 percent in 1958 to 40 percent in 1981. Evangelicals attend church a little more faithfully than do members of the mainline denominations. About 45 percent of the members of evangelical groups may be found in church on a given Sunday. The Midwest leads the nation in percentage of adults attending church on an average Sunday (47%) and is followed by the South (44%), the East (39%), and the West (32%). Canadian attendance has slipped even more than that of the United States, from 60 percent in 1957 to 35 percent in 1982. In Quebec the Catholic church has reported dramatic decline. But the French-speaking evangelical congregations are increasing rapidly. They more than doubled between 1976 and 1982, going from 150 to more than 300 churches in a population of more than 5 million.

The composition of the population of the United States has changed considerably in recent years. A Gallup report covering the period 1947 to 1980 showed Roman Catholics moving from 20 to 29 percent of the population, Protestants slipping from 69 to 59 percent, and Jews slipping from 5 percent to 2 percent. Part of the reason for this shift is the higher birth rate among peoples who are traditionally Catholic, and part of it stems from the tremendous influx of Hispanics.

It is estimated that there are more than 20 million Hispanics in the United States now, making it the fifth largest Spanish-speaking country in the world behind Mexico, Spain, Argentina, and Colombia. Further, it is estimated that 2 million Mexicans slip illegally into the United States annually. Soon Hispanics will surpass blacks as the largest minority bloc in the nation. A majority of Hispanics are unchurched but are nominally Catholic. Tabulations indicate there are about 4 million of them in the Los Angeles area (only about 1 percent of which are evangelical Christian), 2 million in the New York City area, 1 million around Chicago, and a half million in Miami. Jehovah's Witnesses claim some 50,000 Hispanic adherents, Mormons about the same number in the Southwest, Southern Baptists 115,000, and Assemblies of God 66,000.

Many of the old-line denominations are in real trouble in this country. In turning away from a biblically centered message to social action projects and in turning away from standard services to more contemporary approaches, they have alienated masses of people. Of the ten largest Protestant bodies, seven suffered an average loss of 10 percent of their members during the decade of the seventies. More specifically, between 1960 and 1979, the Episcopal Church lost 430,000; the Lutheran Church in America, 130,000; the United Presbyterian Church in the U.S.A., 770,000; the United Church of Christ, 520,000; the Christian Church (Disciples), 570,000; and the United Methodists, 1,150,000. The first five of these denominations lost an additional 200,000 during 1980 alone. The United Methodists lost about 280,000 during the years 1978-1981. All of these have emphasized social action almost to the exclusion of evangelism. Now there are stirrings within these denominations to launch evangelistic efforts. They eye with some jealousy the growth of the conservative denominations.

While liberally oriented American denominations have experienced decline in membership, the United Church of Canada has had the same experience. Membership in 1966 stood at 1,062,000. In 1977 it had declined to 930,000; and in 1982 to 900,000. Since 1975 Sunday school enrollment has fallen by about 60 percent. This augurs ill for the future because it means that the church will not have the recruits needed to maintain the membership in years to come.

During the last decade there has been especially great debate over theological slippage and social and political involvement in four major American denominations: the Presbyterian Church in the U.S. (Southern Presbyterians), the United Methodists, Missouri Synod Lutherans, and the Southern Baptists. Controversy among the Southern Presbyterians led to a defection of 40,000 of them in fourteen states in 1973 to form the Presbyterian Church in America. The new denomination increased to 75,000 to 1980. In 1983 it merged with the Reformed Presbyterian Church-Evangelical Synod, with a combined membership of 130,000 organized in 807 churches and supporting 205 missionaries.

The United Methodist defection has moved in various directions, but some of it resulted in the formation of the Evangelical Church of North America in 1968. That denomination has not grown rapidly; its membership stood at 13,000 last year.

A decade ago the Lutheran Church-Missouri Synod was launched on a doctrinal and political dispute that threatened to wreck the denomination. In 1974 Synod president J. A. O. Preus fired John Tietjen, then president of Concordia Seminary in St. Louis. A total of 45 of the 50 faculty and 400 of the 600 students walked off campus and formed Christ Seminary or Seminex (Seminary-in-Exile). Gradually local churches also broke their ties with the denomination and organized the Association of Evangelical Lutheran Churches, which currently has a membership of 109,000. Seminex has graduated about 700 over the years, most of them entering the ministry of the Association of Evangelical Lutherans; but some took positions in the American Lutheran Church and the Lutheran Church in America. Missouri Synod leaders refused to budge from an avowedly orthodox position. Seminex graduated its last class of 25 in 1983 and closed its doors. Most of the faculty has been assigned to other Lutheran seminaries. The 2.6 million-member Missouri Synod has weathered the storm, has turned back the tide of theological liberalism, and shows few signs of shifting from its staunchly conservative course. Enrollment at Concordia is now about 700, approximately the level it had before the exodus of 1974.

Southern Baptists, like Missouri Synod Lutherans, have been engaging in considerable debate over theological liberalism in their ranks. A very vocal group of adherents to biblical inerrancy has hurled charges of liberalism against the denominational seminaries and has sought to cut off colleges that in the conservatives' view are now so secular as not to be considered church-related any longer. Many churches have withheld contributions from denominational agencies, and some have broken away to organize evangelical fellowships. But evangelicals generally have determined to turn the denomination around. They have managed to elect effective evangelicals to fill the office of president of the Southern Baptist Convention for the last several years. The appointment by these men of theologically-conservative trustees is causing the denomination to make a historic turn to the right. It is difficult to know how far the movement will go. Meanwhile Southern Baptists keep on with aggressive expansion. During 1982 their Sunday school enrollment reached 7,678,607, breaking a record set in 1964; and church membership increased by 1.5 percent to a total of 13,998,252.

Indications of decadence or religious decline in America are evident in the dramatic cut (more than one-third during the last two decades) in the missionary forces supported by the more liberally oriented denominations that are experiencing decline in membership. Moreover, all across the country many old-line denominations have been experiencing sharp declines in seminary enrollments, and some seminaries have merged.

Doctrinal and numerical slippage in many denominations has led to the rise of renewal movements. Two of the most important of them are People for Biblical Witness in the United Church of Christ and the Lay Witness Movement in the United Methodist Church. In 1982 leaders of renewal movements in seven mainline denominations gathered in Pittsburgh to associate themselves into a Fellowship of Renewal Group Leaders. The impact of Inter-Varsity Christian Fellowship and Campus Crusade for Christ nationwide, of Fuller Theological Seminary on the Presbyterian churches of California, and of Gordon-Conwell Theological Seminary on the ministers of New England has been given special credit for the rise of renewal movements.

WOMEN IN THE CHURCH

In many old-line denominations, but unrelated to their decline, there has been a receptiveness to women in places of leadership. They have been ordained as elders and ministers with an increasing frequency. With the exception of some of the Pentecostal and holiness groups, evangelicals generally have not been open to the acceptance of women in places of authority. Roman Catholics refuse to ordain them to the priesthood. The number of women enrolled in seminaries has increased dramatically, and their involvement in Christian education, church music, missions, and other ministries has risen sharply. The United Church of Christ is the first United States denomination to have a female majority (just over half) in its seminaries. Denominations having about one-third women in their seminaries are the Christian Church (Disciples of Christ), United Presbyterian Church, and the United Methodist Church. The American Baptist Church and the Lutheran Church in America have about one-fourth. All branches of Judaism except the Orthodox now ordain women as rabbis.

EVANGELICAL ADVANCE

Within the great denominations and existing as separatist groups are significant and growing numbers of evangelical Christians. This element has become increasingly vocal and respected in recent years. It has benefited greatly from the rehabilitation of the Bible in scholarly circles as a result of Near Eastern Studies. An increasing number of evangelicals have trained in the finest universities of the world and now serve as professors and department heads in the universities. Dozens of fully accredited Christian colleges dot the American countryside; and an Accrediting Association of Bible Colleges has come into being with a growing list of fully accredited and associate members. There are now more than 200 Bible colleges in North America; 68 of them were accredited by the American Association of Bible Colleges as of 1980, with an enrollment of about 30,000. Approximately 75 percent of the evangelical missionaries on the foreign field are Bible college graduates. Evangelical seminaries, instead of withering on the vine, reported expanding and, in some cases, exploding enrollments during the 1970s. But with the smaller number of college graduates, economic recession, and rapidly rising seminary costs during the 1980s, most of those seminaries experienced a leveling off in enrollment or a slight decline. A few of the more successful reported only a slowing in the rate of growth. Nearly all of them were forced to hire admissions recruiters and to increase their advertising budgets. Numerous religious radio stations have been established, and individual programs are aired on national and international hookups. The "electronic church," evangelical telecasting, reaches millions of viewers every week. Again mass evangelism is stirring many of the great cities of the world, especially through the efforts of Billy Graham and his team. Fantastic has been the success of Graham crusades across the United States, Europe, and the Far East.

Church memberships of evangelical groups continue to expand rapidly. In 1982 the Highland Park Baptist Church in Chattanooga, with Lee Roberson as pastor, reported a membership of 54,989. The three next largest churches in the United States in 1982 were the First Baptist of Hammond, Indiana, with Jack Hyles as pastor, 52,355; the First Baptist of Dallas, with W. A. Criswell as pastor, 21,135; and Thomas Road Baptist of Lynchburg, Virginia, with Jerry Falwell as pastor, 17,000. A Gallup poll released in September 1976 indicated that 34 percent of all adult Americans claim to have had a "born again" experience (by projection, some 50 million), and four out of ten believe that "the Bible is to be taken literally, word for word." These are far higher figures than evangelicals ever were willing to claim.

Missionary concern. The missionary concern of the American church and of Christians worldwide has increased tremendously. At home there has been the continuing work of such organizations as the Christian Business Men's Committee, the Christian Business Women's Committee, Inter-Varsity Christian Fellowship, and Child Evangelism, and the phenomenal growth of the newer ministries of Young Life, Youth For Christ, Navigators, and Campus Crusade for Christ and a host of other works too numerous to mention. Many of these agencies are involved in foreign as well as home missions.

Between 1950 and 1970, the number of Protestant career missionaries worldwide increased from 15,000 to 33,000, serving in 130 countries. The number of full-time North American missionaries stationed abroad is currently about 35,000; of these approximately 55 percent are women. In addition, some 20,000 serve under "short term abroad" programs, a new development that permits students, professional or retired people, or others to serve abroad for periods from about three months to two years in length. Many sending agencies report fewer "casualties" on the foreign field in recent years as a result of more careful screening of applicants and better training and counseling programs.

A decline in the number of missionaries sent by agencies affiliated with the National Council of Churches was first noted in 1960. Between 1962 and 1979 the number of foreign missionaries supported by major United States denominations declined by the following percentages: Episcopal, 79; United Presbyterian, 72; Lutheran Church in America, 70; United Church of Christ, 68; Christian Church (Disciples), 66; United Methodist, 46; American Lutheran Church, 44. Overall, the number of missionaries from denominations belonging to the National Council of Churches decreased by 51 percent.

During the same period Southern Baptists increased their missionary force by 88 percent and the Assemblies of God by 49 percent. Agencies affiliated with the Evangelical Foreign Missions Association increased their missionaries on the field by 63 percent; and those affiliated with the Interdenominational Foreign Mission Association increased theirs by 19 percent.

In recent years Third World missionaries have begun to respond to the challenge of the Great Commission in substantial numbers. A 1980 survey revealed that there were 13,000 cross-cultural Third World missionaries; 38 percent were Asian, many representing agencies that were 50 to 75 years old. A 1982 estimate put the total of Third World missionaries at more than 15,000 and concluded that the figure had tripled in eight years. This total represents 368 non-Western mission agencies from at least 57 different countries. More than 5,000 Africans serve as missionaries on their own continent, and there are some 2,700 indigenous Indian missionaries.

An indication of the upsurge in interest in foreign missions was the Inter-Varsity-sponsored Urbana, Illinois, conference in December 1973, which recorded registrations totaling 14,153, the largest student missionary conference in history. The Urbana conference in December 1976 topped that, with an attendance of about 17,000. At Urbana in 1979, 17,500 attended, with more than 8,000 youths indicating they were serious about answering God's call to a missionary vocation. The three-year Urbana cycle was changed to a two-year cycle in 1981 and 14,000 trekked to Urbana. Thereafter Inter-Varsity decided to return to the three-year cycle and to lay plans to hold an urban missions event in the middle of each cycle. A result of that decision was "San Francisco '83: Declaring Christ as Lord in the City."

During the 1982 Christmas holiday over 7,000 young people from about 30 European nations met at Lausanne, Switzerland, under the auspices of the European Missionary Association to think, learn, and pray about missions. Messages were translated into twelve languages for more than 650 missionaries.

To consider ways of fulfilling the Great Commission by the year 2000, 2,700 delegates from around the world met in Lausanne, Switzerland, in July 1974. Half the delegates were from Third World countries. The Lausanne assembly established a Lausanne Committee for World Evangelization that has had a continuing impact. For example, in July 1980 a ten-day conference sponsored by the committee met in Bangkok, Thailand. A total of 650 participants from 87 countries met in a working consultation to evaluate "where we are" in the task of reaching the world's 3 billion non-Christians with the gospel. And on April 23, 1982, the Confraternity of Evangelicals in Latin America organized in Panama City, Panama, under the auspices of the Lausanne Committee.

New approaches in missions. The new approach in foreign missions today is not to concentrate so much on pioneer evangelism, but on the use of all God-given talents in the spread of the gospel. This is true not only because this is the wisest plan that could be adopted, but also because it is necessary. Churches abroad have come of age. Nationalistic fervor in the Third World requires that national churches be free to chart their own destinies. In recent years more and more mission property has been deeded over to national churches with control in the hands of national workers. Missionaries become fraternal workers and provide support or technical know-how for churches abroad. Of special importance is the providing of training for foreign nationals so they can more effectively evangelize their own people. The world is being blanketed with a network of Bible schools. And as university training abroad has become available to a larger number of Christians, seminary programs have been instituted in country after country. An example of the new educational opportunities now offered in Europe is the operation of nine Greater Europe Mission Bible institutes all across the continent. The Greater Europe Mission is launching a graduate school of theology, Tyndale Theological Seminary, in the Netherlands in 1984, which will join their already-established German Theological Seminary.

New techniques in missions are speeding the message on its way and making existing work more effective. Missionary radio has virtually blanketed the globe and some television programming is now being offered. The great pioneer in the field is HCJB in Quito, Ecuador; but there is a host of others, including ELWA in Liberia, TGNA in Guatemala, CP-27 in Bolivia, WIVV in Puerto Rico, Far Eastern Broadcasting Company in the Philippines, Korea, and the Seychelles, and Trans World Radio with transmitters in Monaco, Bonaire, Swaziland, and Sri Lanka. Access to secular stations in Western Europe is increasing. For example in France over 300 independent radio stations have been established since François Mitterand's Socialist government came to power. Some of these have been willing to broadcast Christian programs. The government-controlled television network is now airing programs for Christian groups. In Spain evangelicals have had some access to state radio and TV since 1982.

In 1980 Christian radio and television stations worldwide were said to number 1,450. By far the largest single bloc is located in the United States. In late 1983 there were 922 radio stations and 65 TV stations owned and operated by evangelicals in the United States, according to National Religious Broadcasters. Though stations come and go, new Christian radio stations have been formed in the United States at the rate of about one per week and television stations at the rate of about one per month since 1975.

Religious TV in the United States grew steadily through the

fifties and sixties and exploded in the first half of the seventies. By 1970 there were 38 syndicated television programs. By 1975, when growth leveled off, the number had reached 65. In 1972 Pat Robertson operated the only religious TV station in the United States. In 1983 the number of such stations had reached 65, as noted. Of the major producers of American religious telecasts, a 1983 Arbitron rating service survey put Robert Schuller at the head of the list with an audience of 2,667,000; Jimmy Swaggart second with 2,653,000; and Oral Roberts, Rex Humbard, and Jerry Falwell in third, fourth, and fifth spots. An Arbitron rating for the previous year had put Oral Roberts, Rex Humbard, Robert Schuller, and Jerry Falwell in the top four spots, the first three with more than 2 million viewers each.

The entire religious TV audience in the United States is variously rated at 10 million, 14 million, and 20-22 million; and it is believed that as many as half the nation may watch a religious special, such as a Billy Graham crusade. But there is increasing competition within the field of religious broadcasters, and Sunday morning competition with news broadcasts and movie offerings is making life harder for religious broadcasters.

Religious TV is making a significant impact in Japan (where over 98 percent have color TV), which has long resisted traditional methods of evangelism. Taking a lead in the religious programming is the Christian Broadcasting Network (CBN) and Living Bibles International. These two agencies also cooperate in promoting programs in Korea, Taiwan, and Hong Kong. CBN has also launched TV programs in numerous countries of Europe, Africa, the Philippines, and Canada.

Missionary aviation is also coming into its own. Missionary Aviation Fellowship was organized in 1944 and now has a plane taking off every five or six minutes on the average, around the clock, every day of the year, somewhere in the world. Wycliffe Bible Translators is another agency using airplanes in a major way through its aviation arm, JAARS. The Moody Bible Institute aviation course especially contributes to training pilots for missionary work.

Another specialty ministry is Gospel Recordings, Inc., which is producing Bible stories and basic Christian teaching in a very

large percentage of the languages and dialects of the world. It has
been successful in recording materials for use among peoples
who as yet have not had their languages put into writing.

Colportage work and Bible correspondence course programs
abound everywhere. The kind of ministry conducted by the
Moody Correspondence School (with more than ninety-two thousand enrollments) is being performed by an increasing number
of other schools in many places around the world. Numerous
schools are grading scores of thousands of papers every month.
Home Bible-study classes are one of the greatest phenomena of
the hour; no one knows how many scores of thousands there are
in this country—stimulated by the work of the Navigators, Campus Crusade for Christ, local churches, and other agencies. And
they are taking hold everywhere abroad. Often this is the only
way Christians can function behind the iron curtain. Religious
journalism is a new hope for Christian evangelism. The *Envol*
publications make their way in Zaire, *Africa Challenge* elsewhere
in Africa, and *Dengta* in Hong Kong—to note a few of the successful magazines published on the field.

Scripture distribution. A very important phase of mission work
worldwide is Scripture distribution. The Wycliffe Bible Translators, formally organized in 1942, is dedicated to the task of reducing to writing all the languages of the world and translating at
least portions of the Bible into those languages. As of 1983, at
least one book of the Bible had been published in 1,763 languages used by 97 percent of the world's people. This compares
with portions of the Bible available in only 67 languages at the
beginning of the twentieth century. Wycliffe translation programs
presently are working on 1,200 new languages, and staff members begin work on a new language every 13 days. It takes about
15 years of work for two persons to accomplish the Wycliffe goal
of reducing a language to writing and translating a portion of
Scripture into that language. Wycliffe can vouch for the existence
of 5,171 separate language groups, and the total increases each
year. Some indication of the magnitude of the task is seen in a
report that although there was rejoicing over completion of the
translation of the New Testament into the language of the Soviet
Union's 3.5 million Georgians in 1980, no part of the Bible had

yet been translated into 90 of the 127 main languages of the Soviet Union. Wycliffe now has 4,255 staff members, making it the largest independent mission in history. More than 18,000 have attended Wycliffe's Summer Institute of Linguistics training program.

Numerous agencies and individuals are involved in Scripture distribution. The Gideons give out a million Bibles or Testaments every 17 days. During the reporting year ending May 31, 1983, the 60,000-member organization gave away 22,200,000 Bibles and Testaments in about 135 countries and 60 languages. The American Bible Society distributed its 3 billionth copy of Scripture in 1979; that year was the 164th anniversary of the founding of the Society in 1816. During 1979 the Society distributed 258,939,314 Scriptures worldwide. For that year total distribution of the United Bible Societies (of which ABS is a member) worldwide was almost 500 million Bibles and portions. For 1982 the ABS distributed 244 million and the United Bible Societies almost 485 million Bibles and portions. The Pocket Testament League is also very busy disseminating the Bible. For the year ending in September 1982, the League distributed 500,000 Scripture portions in the United States, including 95,000 New Testaments on thirty college campuses. Its staff of about 100 is active in Scripture distribution and evangelism in numerous other countries; for example, during 1982 staff members gave away 135,000 Scripture portions in Brazil, 100,000 in Spain, and 95,000 in Indonesia. The International Bible Society, formerly the New York International Bible Society, distributed 6,278,656 Bibles worldwide during the year ending June 30, 1983. Almost all of these were in the society's translation, the *New International Version*. Of special interest is a news note from the American Bible Society that more than 50 million Scripture portions were distributed in India in 1982, "a remarkable record considering there are less than half that number of Christians in India."

Scripture distribution behind the Iron and Bamboo curtains is tightly controlled, but occasionally communist governments make gestures toward the local populace or world opinion. For example, in 1980 the Chinese government permitted the printing of 50,000 Chinese New Testaments; and the Bible suddenly became the most sought-after book in the country. In 1981, 20,000 Bibles and 20,000 hymnals arrived in Haiphong harbor aboard a Russian freighter. Printed by the Federation of Protestant churches in East Germany, these were destined for the churches of Vietnam. In 1982, 195,000 Bibles were printed in Poland; and in addition the Bible Society in Poland arranged the import of 50,000 pocket-sized Bibles. During the same year Soviet authorities gave permission for the annual printing of 10,000 Bibles, 10,000 New Testaments, and 10,000 hymnals. Also during 1982 the American Bible Society sent Bibles and portions to communist Eastern Europe through cooperating agencies in the following numbers: Soviet Union, 10,000 (New Testaments); Yugoslavia, 44,000; Romania, 50,000 (Bibles); Poland, 176,000; East Germany, 402,631; and Hungary, 37,000.

A phenomenon of recent years has been the reception accorded Kenneth Taylor's *Living Bible*, annually being printed by the millions in dozens of languages. As an indication of its outreach, recently 360,000 Thai *Living New Testaments* were distributed in Thailand. In addition, the *New American Standard Bible*, the *Good News Bible*, the *New International Version*, the *New English Bible*, the *New Scofield Reference Bible*, the *Ryrie Study Bible*, and the *New King James Version* have sparked new interest in the abiding Word of God.

RESPONSE TO THE GOSPEL

It is now time to ask what kind of response the gospel is receiving in the world in this supposedly post-Christian era. In comments that follow there is room for only a few tantalizing examples of what God is doing. As this is being written it appears there are more Christians in the emerging countries than in Europe and North America. More than one American denomination has been impressed and a little embarrassed watching work it launched in Africa or Latin America outstripping the founding church in size. Numerically at least the future of the church lies with the black and brown peoples of the world. If present trends continue, by the year 2000 only about 40 percent or less of the Christians of the world will be white.

Behind the Iron Curtain. Behind the Iron Curtain are real signs of life, not only in Russia but in most of the satellite countries of Eastern Europe. In Russia it is estimated that there are some 100 million Christians of all varieties—or about 37 percent of the population. Of these about 70 million are Russian Orthodox; the rest are Armenian Orthodox, Roman Catholics, and Protestants. There are two Protestant groups in the country: the All-Union Council of Evangelical Christians-Baptists (registered with the authorities) and the Council of Churches of Evangelical Christians-Baptists (which has refused to register with the government and is persecuted). It is difficult to quantify evangelical strength in the Soviet Union; but responses to evangelical broadcasts beamed into the country, participation in correspondence courses, the desire for Bibles and other Christian literature, and tabulations of reports of overflowing churches and underground house churches indicate the church is experiencing considerable growth despite all efforts to stifle it.

Since before the middle of the 1970s there have been mounting reports of spiritual awakening all over Eastern Europe. If a free flow of information were possible, the Western church probably would be tremendously impressed by what is going on. In spite of decades of government oppression in East Germany, more than 55 percent of the population is still on the church rolls. This includes 8 million claimed by the main Lutheran body (the Federation of Evangelical Churches), 1.3 million Roman Catholics, 35,000 evangelical Methodists, and 21,000 Baptists. A charismatic renewal movement is now sweeping the East German Lutheran church; about 10 percent of the clergy, or about 400 pastors, are said to be involved in it. Some indication of the magnitude of religious stirring in East Germany is provided by the Bible distribution figures noted above.

In Poland government oppression and propaganda also have failed to turn the nation to atheism. The vast majority of the people remain staunch Roman Catholics; one report lists 97 percent of the population as at least nominally Roman Catholic. There are reports of considerable spiritual awakening within Polish Catholicism; and Bible distribution is reaching significant proportions. Throughout the decade of the seventies, reports of revival in Romania have been recorded. The Baptists have especially benefited. As the revival has heightened, the government has tightened the screws of persecution. In Hungary as well, the populace refuses to be cowed by atheistic pressures. Over half hold Christian beliefs and about one-third of adults attend church regularly. In 1980 the government approved the teaching of the Bible as literature to 80,000 high school students in an agreement worked out with Roman Catholic, Lutheran, and Calvinist churches. This is a unique development in communist East Europe. It is hard to get a clear picture of what is going on in Czechoslovakia, but evidently spiritual revitalization is so extensive there that the government has determined to wipe out the multitude of Bible study and prayer groups that seem to be meeting in secret all over the country. As noted above, secret agents have been trained to hunt these out, especially groups meeting in the Slovakian mountains.

Behind the Bamboo Curtain. Rips are beginning to appear in the Bamboo Curtain. In spite of Chinese government attacks on Christianity ever since the communist takeover in 1949, and in spite of the especially virulent effort of the Cultural Revolution (1965-68) to exterminate Christianity, the church has survived in China. The government officially recognizes both Roman Catholic and Protestant churches, the former known as the Catholic Patriotic Society and the latter as the Three-Self Churches (self-government, self-propagation, self-support). The Northeastern Theological Seminary (Protestant) opened in a suburb of Peking in November of 1982 with a first class of 50. Previously a Catholic seminary had opened with 36 students.

Five large churches opened again in Shanghai in 1981, and all have over 2,000 in attendance; in the same year the Chinese government permitted a band of Christians to travel from Peking to the Great Wall to hold an Easter sunrise service. More and more Three-Self churches are being permitted to open, and there are now over 700 of them. As the Three-Self movement is allowed to expand, there is increasing persecution of the unofficial house churches that resist registration with the government and governmental interference with their faith. Jonathan Chao, dean of China Graduate School of Theology in Hong Kong, is launch-

ing a "Seminary of the Air" and beaming it into China to provide
a program of instruction for leaders of house churches. He be-
lieves there may be a million such leaders ministering to perhaps
25 million believers. The Hong Kong-based Chinese Church Research Center estimates that 15 counties in Honan province have
an average of 100,000 Christians worshiping in house churches.
If that is true, the population of the province must be at least 2
percent Christian.

Christianity is making progress in the "other Chinas" too. It is
estimated to command the allegiance of more than 800,000 (two-
thirds of which are Protestant) or about 5 percent of the population of Taiwan. Hong Kong is believed to be about 10 percent
Christian, as is Singapore, in the Chinese "dispersion."

In Communist Vietnam (as of 1983) there are an estimated
200,000 in the evangelical church of the south, but only 10,000 or
less in the north.

Africa. From Africa comes a seemingly never-ending tale of
spiritual movement. One report estimates that Christians are increasing twice as fast as the continent's total population. Another
claims that 1,000 new churches are being organized every Sunday, that 52,000 are being converted every day, and that the continent will be 46 percent evangelical Christian by the year 2000. In
Marxist-controlled Mozambique a 1983 report indicated that
churches formerly affiliated with the Africa Evangelical Fellowship multiplied tenfold to 44,000 baptized believers in 450
churches during the twenty years of rigid control. The gospel
continues to enjoy great receptivity in Marxist-controlled Ethiopia as well. In one church alone in the capital of Addis Ababa,
670 professions of faith were reported in late 1982. In Marxist-led
Zimbabwe a revival has been sweeping the government schools.
At the beginning of 1983, 5,500 professions of faith by children
twelve years and older had been reported.

Though several Bible institutes have existed in Africa for many
years, the maturing of the church there increasingly has required
graduate-level seminary training. To meet the need, the Bangui
Evangelical School of Theology in the Central African Republic
was founded in 1977. This is the first evangelical seminary in
Africa under the auspices of the Association of Evangelicals of

Africa and Madagascar (AEAM). The school has an enrollment of about 50, and graduated its first class of 14 in June of 1982. The Evangelical Churches of West Africa launched a seminary at Jos, Nigeria, in 1980 to complement an already existing seminary founded by the Sudan Interior Mission in Igbaja, southern Nigeria. Each accommodates about 40 students.

The Muslim world. Establishing and building the church in a Muslim land is one of the most difficult tasks faced by Christian missionaries today, and some Muslim countries have no organized group of believers. But there are some signs of spiritual life in the Muslim world. There is a report of the moving of the Holy Spirit in Egypt in recent years, especially among Christian Copts; and a significant number of Bible study groups reportedly meet in homes in the Cairo area. Grace Church of Edina, Minnesota, has a center in Cairo where in 1982 over 2,800 Egyptians learned how to introduce others to Christ and how to lead small group Bible studies. Presumably this effort will make an impact in years to come. The work of God goes on in Lebanon, especially among the Christian minority, in spite of the vicissitudes of war. Reports coming out of Iran indicate that the church there continues to function, in spite of all the pressure exerted against it. The Iranian Bible Society recently distributed 30,000 booklets entitled "Drugs, the Shadow of Death." These contain Scripture verses intended to help addicts in their struggle to overcome their addiction.

Of special interest is the revival in Indonesia. After the 1965 revolution, which became violently anti-Communist, revival broke out on one after the other of the Indonesian islands, notably North Sumatra, Java, and Timor. After 1970 the mass movements of new converts into the churches slowed, but Java experienced another sweeping revival in 1972. On Timor, 200,000 baptisms occurred in 1965 and 1966 alone. Between 1964 and 1971, Protestant church membership doubled from 4 to over 8 million in a nation of 119 million. There have been so many conversions that some areas are predominantly Christian in this Muslim land. Gospel advertisements in Muslim newspapers of Indonesia in 1975 resulted in 21,000 enrolling in Bible correspondence courses and 3,400 making decisions for Christ. World Vision reported a combined attendance of 250,000 in a 1976 crusade in Kupang, Indonesia, with throngs of inquirers responding to the invitation.

Korea. South Korea seems to be involved in a continuing revival. The Korean Protestant community approximately doubled its size during each decade from 1940 to 1970 and tripled it during the 1970s. In 1940 there were about 370,000; in 1950, 600,000; in 1960, 1.34 million; in 1970, 2.25 million; and in 1979, 7 million. Thus Christians now constitute about 20 percent of the population of 38 million. Korea's Christian population grows four times as fast as the total national population. One estimate claims that six new churches are formed every day. Protestants outnumber Roman Catholics six to one and about half of the Protestants are Presbyterian. Korea International Mission, founded in 1968, is a leader in Third World Missions. Korea now has 10 Protestant colleges and universities, 40 Bible schools, and 70 seminaries. In all the nation's universities and colleges there are now more students than in the universities of England.

In Korean Christianity the extraordinary becomes almost ordinary, or at least repeatable and capable of being improved on. Billy Graham preached to 1.1 million in the concluding service of his Seoul crusade in 1973. Explo '74, in Seoul, had over a million in attendance at one meeting. In that year, a reported 35 percent of the South Korean army was Christian. In August of 1980 the World Evangelization Crusade met in Seoul as part of the total Christianization movement of the country. It was sponsored by 19 denominations. On the final night there was a crowd of 3 million (in a city of 8 million), and 2 million or more attended two of the four evening sessions preceding the final one. Five all-night prayer meetings continued until 5:00 A.M., with a combined attendance of 600,000. The basic stress of the crusade was on missions, and during the crusade 10,000 university and 3,000 high school students committed themselves to missions. At the last service a declaration was read committing the entire gathering to the use of the Korean church's resources for world evangelization.

The most remarkable feature of Korea's Christian community is Paul Cho's Full Gospel Central Church in Seoul. In 1983 it had

350,000 members with a goal of 500,000 in 1984. Some 13,000 of his members spend all Friday night in prayer. On Sundays several services are held in the auditorium, which can accommodate 20,000; and huge Sunday schools meet simultaneously in other facilities.

Three major reasons are given for the unparalleled success of the church in South Korea: (1) a wise noncolonialist missionary program that has stressed evangelism, self-support, and the training of the whole body of believers in study of the Bible; (2) steadfastness of believers under persecution; and (3) the impact of the revival of 1907-1908.

Japan. There are only about one million baptized Christians in a population of 118 million in Japan, and there were more baptized Christians in proportion to the population 350 years ago than now. But there are signs of change. The militant Buddhist sect of Soka Gakkai, once considered a major threat to Christian expansion, has been discredited by scandal and its membership has been cut in half in recent years. There is a new spirit in Japan that may hold promise for Christianity. Many are hopeful that Christian television programs will be effective in evangelization. In 1978 for the first time Japan had a Christian prime minister, Masayoshi Ohira. When he died in 1980, the cross was prominently displayed at his widely televised funeral.

The Philippines. In 1981 a two-day congress of 488 evangelical leaders representing 81 denominations and parachurch organizations committed themselves to a plan to establish an evangelical church in every ward of the Philippines by the year 2000. This plan to "disciple a nation" would require increasing the existing 10,000 congregations to 50,000.

This concept of having a church within easy reach of everyone in the country was launched by the 60 Filipino delegates to Lausanne in 1974. Spot checks of 12 denominations in 1978 showed that between 1974 and 1978 there had been an almost sixfold increase in those groups. The 12 denominations surveyed were growing at a rate that would enable them to exceed the goal by the year 2000, and there are 75 denominations in the country. The Christian and Missionary Alliance alone is projecting an annual growth rate of 15 percent during the target period, with an increase from a membership of 60,000 in 900 churches to 2 million in 20,000 churches. If the goal is reached, the present 1 million evangelicals will grow to 4 or 5 million and will equal 6 to 8 percent of an expected population of 80 million by 2000. Perhaps the Philippines will establish an example that will provide a beacon light for the entire world.

Latin America. God is at work in Latin America. Over five thousand new evangelical churches were established in the region in 1974. In that year on December 15, 20,000 people jammed the Jotabeche Pentecostal Methodist Church in Santiago, Chile, for its dedication. The largest evangelical church in the world at that time, it had 80,000 members. Members attend the mother church once a month and one of the one hundred branch churches on other Sundays. An important event of 1973 was the preaching of twenty-one-year-old Julio César Ruibal in Colombia and Bolivia. Over 70,000 came to hear him in the soccer stadium in Medellin, Colombia; it was reported to be the largest crowd ever in that city. In the same year David Wilkerson reported that the Jesus revolution was sweeping the high school and college campuses of Brazil. Brazil now has an especially large evangelical community. In 1983 the First Baptist Church of Sao Paulo regularly had about 20,000 in attendance on a Sunday. Child Evangelism and Word of Life staff members are among those teaching required Bible classes in the public schools of the country. The Graham crusade in Rio de Janeiro, Brazil (1974), packed 225,000 into the stadium on the closing day, and television carried Graham's message to the entire nation on that occasion. In 1976 Argentine evangelist Luis Palau had an especially successful crusade in Asuncion, Paraguay. About 10,000 gathered nightly during the twelve-day crusade, and 5,000 made professions of faith. There had been only 3,000 evangelicals in the city before that time.

In spite of all the unrest in Central America, evangelical expansion goes on effectively. Evangelical Protestants in Nicaragua are now said to number about 400,000 in a population of 2.7 million. During 1979-83, under the Sandinista regime, the distribution of Bibles increased fivefold and the distribution of New Testaments ninefold.

Estimates put the evangelical community in Guatemala at over 1 million, or 15-20 percent of the population at the 100th anniversary of the first coming of Protestant missionaries in 1882. Some claim that at the present rate of growth evangelicals could constitute about 50 percent of the population by 1990. Caution is in order when such claims are made for developing countries, because a very large percentage of the population consists of children; in Guatemala 45 percent of the population is aged 14 and below. Over 6,000 are regularly in attendance on a Sunday at the Elim Church, an independent Pentecostal church in Guatemala City. About 80 percent of Guatemala's evangelicals are Pentecostal. The largest crowd ever to turn out for an evangelical preacher in Central America came to hear Luis Palau in Guatemala City on November 28, 1982; it was variously estimated at between 350,000 and 700,000 persons. Over 3,000 decisions were registered during the eight-day campaign. Guatemala City has a Bible institute with about 250 students and the Central American Theological Seminary with about 100 students.

The number of Protestant believers in Central America has doubled or tripled between 1970 and 1980, according to figures compiled by the Institute of In-Depth Evangelism of San Jose, Costa Rica. This same rate of growth apparently holds true for Mexico. There evangelicals were said to number 900,000 (1.8 percent of the population) in 1970 and 2.4 million (3.5 percent of the population) in 1980. One report projects that for all Latin America, memberships of evangelical churches are growing over three times faster than the general population. This phenomenon has worried Roman Catholics, and a recent conference of bishops zeroed in on rapid evangelical growth and sought ways to combat it. It is thought that likely elements of Roman Catholic response will include more aggressive use of radio and television, more use of the Bible in teaching, and more singing in church services.

Trends in the Latin American church include continued growth of the charismatic movement, explosive increase of independent groups, modification of worship models, and a new ecumenicity. There is rapid growth of the charismatic movement inside and outside the Roman church. Some 75-80 percent of

Latin American Protestants are Pentecostal. There is an explosion of new church bodies completely separate from North American mission ties; for example, there are reportedly about 40 independent bodies in Guatemala and 190 in Nicaragua. There is a development of new worship models that are non-North American and more fitted to the Latin context.

The new ecumenicity among Latin American Protestants became very visible on April 23, 1982, when the Confraternity of Evangelicals in Latin America (CONELA) was organized in Panama City under the impetus and auspices of the Lausanne Committee for World Evangelization. Ninety-eight Protestant denominations and seventy-four Christian service agencies participated in the event. Designed to facilitate communication among conservative evangelicals rather than to be a decision-making body, the continent-wide alliance will hold the line for conservative, biblical evangelicals. Since its organization CONELA has had wide reception and support across the region. A rider to the constitution declared that CONELA would not join either the World Council of Churches or the International Christian Council. The Confraternity was designed to be an alternative to the Latin American Council of Churches (CLAI), which has ties to the World Council of Churches.

Pentecostal ministry. As noted above, much of the revival movement in Latin America is led by Pentecostals, who especially appeal to the masses and who have been successful in building large churches all over South America. Pentecostals have been active almost everywhere else around the world, too. For instance, as of 1976 they had established 200 churches in Thailand with 6,000 members. And they have been heavily involved in the Indonesian revival. Moreover, the charismatic movement has invaded all segments of the American church, but has made a special impact on the Anglican and Roman Catholic churches. In fact, charismatic Roman Catholics may now be found all over the world. In the spring of 1976, 35,000 of them braved a weekend of rain in Notre Dame's football stadium to attend a conference on the Holy Spirit. In the fall of 1977, 37,000 Roman Catholic charismatics met in Atlantic City. Earlier that year 50,000 charismatics of various faiths met in a week-long conference in

Kansas City. And in the spring of 1978, 54,000 charismatics rallied in the Meadowlands Stadium of Rutherford, New Jersey. A tabulation completed in 1978 reported that 8 million American Roman Catholics were Pentecostals. At the same time, there were 3.2 million black Pentecostals in the United States. The fastest-growing denomination in America is the 1.6 million-member Assemblies of God. Its membership cuts across all social classes and claims such leaders as James Watt, former Secretary of the Interior, and Missouri Attorney General John Ashcroft.

The Catholic charismatic movement is especially strong in Peru. In Lima alone there are some 30,000 who meet in about 150 prayer groups. Adherents are drawn from the upper class, whereas evangelical Protestants come largely from the lower classes. This movement does not emphasize speaking in tongues. The charismatic crusade in Lima really took off in 1979, after the Sixth Catholic Charismatic Encounter in Latin America (ECCLA VI) met in the city for ten days with some 90 delegates who were leaders of the Catholic renewal in 20 countries of the Americas. Their emphasis was evangelization of Latin America's 300 million baptized Catholics.

The thirteenth World Pentecostal Conference convened in Nairobi, Kenya, in September 1982, with 11,000 participants. The conference met in spite of the uncertainties connected with the attempted coup against Kenyan president Daniel Moi, an evangelical Christian. Moi addressed the group, 90 percent of whom were black. More would have attended from abroad if the coup attempt had not taken place. It is estimated that there are now some 100 million Pentecostals in the world: about 51 million in Pentecostal groups worldwide outside of Africa, 11 million in the traditional churches, and the rest in the mushrooming African independent churches. For example, one must take account of the 5-million-member Kimbanguist Church of Zaire and the 1.2 million Pentecostals of Kenya.

The Pentecostal Resource Center has just been completed near the Church of God headquarters in Cleveland, Tennessee. Designed to house an array of data on the Pentecostal movement, the 2.5 million dollar structure will be a valuable resource to researchers and writers.

The Jews. One of the most exciting developments of our ti
the inroads of the gospel among the Jews. The leader in the fie
of Jewish missions today is Jews for Jesus (an outgrowth of the
Jesus movement of the sixties), which was founded in 1973.
Moishe Rosen is executive director of the organization. Jews for
Jesus maintains its headquarters in San Francisco; has main
offices in New York City, Boston, and Chicago; branches in Miami, Toronto, and Los Angeles; and chapters manned by volunteers in 37 other cities. Jews for Jesus is especially known for its
communications techniques, which may include anything from
full-page ads in the *Wall Street Journal* to preaching on street
corners. The group originated Jewish gospel music and maintains three traveling music groups: the Liberated Wailing Wall in
the East, Allelujah in the Chicago area, and Israelite on the West
Coast. The New Jerusalem Players is the Jews for Jesus drama
team.

Jews for Jesus is the largest independent mission to the Jews
and currently has over 100 missionaries on the staff. Second in
size is the Friends of Israel; and third is the American Board of
Missions to the Jews. Among denominational agencies with Jewish missions, the largest is the Assemblies of God, followed by
Baptist Mid-Missions and the Conservative Baptists.

Moishe Rosen gives a figure of 4,300 documented conversions
through the efforts of his mission and estimates that there may be
60,000 Jews in the United States who were born into practicing
Jewish households and have been converted to Christianity. He is
especially encouraged by the rejuvenation and creative vitality of
Jewish missions today. He remarks that Jewish missionaries are
of higher quality now.

Jewish organizations and individual rabbis have sought to dis-
credit Jewish converts to Christianity, accusing them of having
emotional or home problems, of being weak-minded, of coming
from families not affiliated with Jewish communal life, and of
being impressionable students who have succumbed to Christian
propaganda. Rosen has set out to get the truth about these
charges, conducting surveys in 1972, 1978, and 1983. The last
survey confirms findings of the two earlier ones. The 1983 survey
was sent out on a random basis to 8,000 converted Jews, and the

returned were used for a data base. Some of ant findings are the following: 72 percent of e in the 25-44 age bracket, not teenagers or e average number of years of education was 15; ted to be identified as Jewish as well as Christian; 32 percent used their occupations in the professional and technical category; and 62 percent said that the agent that influenced their decision was an individual person (clearly not brainwashing by an organization).

The ministry of Billy Graham. No account of the contemporary church would be complete without at least a brief word about Billy Graham. He acquired national fame in 1949 with his first Los Angeles crusade, and world fame in 1954 with his first Greater London crusade. After that year, he crusaded with song leader Cliff Barrows and singer George Beverly Shea and others in most parts of the world. In spite of the massive scale of Graham's campaigns, emphasis is on individual conversion. And once individuals are converted, they are followed up and urged to affiliate with a local church.

Through the ministry of the crusade, Graham has preached the gospel to some 60 million persons, with about 2 million responding for counseling. Since 1950 "The Hour of Decision" radio program has been beamed around the world every Sunday, crossing all kinds of barriers, even into the communist world. Currently the program is aired over 500 stations. In 1982 a 15-minute broadcast in Spanish was added. It is aired in 20 United States cities in which 11 million Spanish-speaking people live.

Approximately 2.5 million copies of *Decision* magazine are distributed worldwide monthly from offices in ten countries. The magazine is also produced in braille. Graham's best sellers, *Peace with God, World Aflame,* and *Angels,* have been another important part of his impact. The film ministry of the Billy Graham Evangelistic Association, World Wide Pictures, has produced over 100 films, among the most effective of which have been *Joni, The Hiding Place,* and *Reflections of His Love.* These films have been shown to well more than 50 million persons with more than 1.5 million inquiring for spiritual guidance. The Association's World Emergency Fund has assisted many victims of catastrophes, such as the Vietnamese boat people, Cambodian refugees, the starving in Africa, and earthquake victims in Guatemala.

The Billy Graham Center at Wheaton College, Wheaton, Illinois, was born out of the desire to make world evangelism the primary concern of Christians today. The Center houses archives, a library of materials on evangelism and missions, and the Wheaton College Graduate School.

To further the cause of evangelism, Graham called an International Conference for Itinerant Evangelists in Amsterdam for ten days beginning on July 11, 1983. Over 3,500 evangelists came from 133 countries—70 percent from the Third World—for instruction and inspiration.

Luis Palau. Luis Palau is sometimes called the Billy Graham of Latin America or a Third World evangelist; but actually he has now become an evangelist to the whole world. Born in Argentina, Palau began his evangelistic crusades in Latin America in 1966. He has been conducting crusades in English for nearly ten years and now has preached about 100 crusades. Of course most of Palau's campaigns have been in Latin America. Reference has already been made to his 1976 crusade in Asuncion, Paraguay, and his 1982 successes in Guatemala. Other examples include his 1980 crusade in Guayaquil, Ecuador, and his 1982 effort in Paraguay. The former was a two-week crusade with a nightly attendance of 6,000 and 2,850 making Christian commitments. The latter was conducted in cooperation with four associate evangelists in seven Paraguayan cities, with a cumulative attendance of 155,000. On the final night, with 25,000 in attendance in the capital, 1,700 made decisions for Christ. Palau's concern for Latins in the United States led him to conduct his first American Spanish-language crusade in the Los Angeles Sports Arena, June 28 to July 6, 1980. Working with a base of about 1 percent evangelicals in a nominally Catholic and largely unchurched Spanish population, he drew an aggregate attendance of 52,000, with about 1,950 making decisions of some sort. Examples of his ministry in Europe have been noted in references to his Helsinki and London crusades. His five-week campaign in Glasgow, Scotland in 1981 also was significant.

Christian literature. Another facet of the work and success of the Christian church today is Christian literature. Whether one considers the books of Billy Graham, James Dobson, Charles Swindoll, Francis Schaeffer, Hal Lindsey, Elisabeth Elliot, or scores and scores of others, he sees that both popular and more scholarly Christian literature from secular houses and the growing number of evangelical publishers has made a profound impact in most parts of the world. And of course Christian magazines such as *Christianity Today, Christian Herald, Moody Monthly, Eternity, Campus Life,* and others all play their parts.

Campus Ministries. The old veteran in the field of campus ministries is Inter-Varsity Christian Fellowship. It had its beginnings in Britain in the 1860s and 1870s. From there it spread to Canada and from Canada came to the United States in 1937. Inter-Varsity was organized in the United States in 1941, and in 1948 C. Stacey Woods (who had been responsible for its establishment in the United States) was instrumental in organizing the International Fellowship of Evangelical Students (IFES), of which the United States' Inter-Varsity is a member. There are now IFES affiliates in about 75 countries, and the coordinating office is in London. IFES affiliates have chapters on 3,200 college and university campuses worldwide.

In the United States more than 400 full-time staff members serve 905 college and university chapters. In addition, Inter-Varsity has a rapidly expanding book publishing division and produces *His* magazine. As previously noted, it organizes triennial missions conferences at Urbana, Illinois, and a series of urban and vocational conferences to prepare students for effective witness on the job. In addition it has four campgrounds for summer training and weekend retreats.

One of the most dynamic and most effective agencies in the outreach of the church today is Campus Crusade for Christ. Founded in 1951 by Bill Bright, it sought first to reach American campuses through use of the "four spiritual laws." In connection with that ministry, it has worked effectively on the beaches of Florida to evangelize students there and has branched out to include ministries to athletes, military men, high school students, and others. In 1982 Campus Crusade had about 16,000 full time and associate staff working in 150 countries and protectorates around the world. The 1,000 field staff in the United States conducted evangelism and discipleship ministry on 250 campuses.

The film *Jesus* is Crusade's greatest single evangelism tool. Based on the gospel of Luke, it is now available in 60 languages and is viewed by about 350,000 per day with reports of phenomenal success in terms of decisions for Christ. "Here's Life" campaigns have been launched in various countries in saturation evangelism programs. A good example of the latter was the 1982 effort in the Netherlands. In March a 48-page magazine entitled *There Is Hope (Er Is Hoop)* was distributed to each of the 5.2 million households in the Netherlands, marking the beginning of the nationwide "Here's Life" campaign. Trained church members have committed themselves to contacting every home in the country during the next two years.

A major American effort of Campus Crusade during 1983 was KC '83, a post-Christmas conference in Kansas City designed to stimulate college students to revolutionize their campuses for Christ. A total of 19,000 attended. Athletes in Action is a sports ministry conducted by Christian athletes under sponsorship of Crusade. The program has been functioning for fifteen years now. It is the goal of Campus Crusade to reach at least one billion people for Christ during the 1980s. It is estimated that all but 1,600-1,800 American campuses have either Inter-Varsity or Campus Crusade ministries on them.

Social involvement. As the evangelical church has presented its message in recent years, it has been increasingly concerned with social action, but tied to the gospel. For a long time the church has been concerned with social involvement in foreign missionary work and thus built hospitals, schools, and other institutions for social betterment. At home too, evangelicals have engaged in a considerable amount of social work. But under the prodding of liberals and many from within the ranks, they have demonstrated a larger and more active social interest through the work of a host of new organizations, such as World Vision,

Food for the Hungry, Farms, the Social Action Committee of the National Association of Evangelicals, the Evangelical Child Welfare Agency, and the Institute for International Development.

DOCTRINAL DEVELOPMENTS

An answer to what is going on in the church must concern more than growth or decline or the success of its mission in the world. What has happened to beliefs and attitudes within the church during this century? To begin with, the departure from conservative theology became more pronounced during the early years of the century. One effort to combat this tendency was the publication of a twelve-volume paperback set produced under the successive editorship of A. C. Dixon, Louis Meyer, and R. A. Torrey (1910-12). Called *The Fundamentals*, these books especially upheld the virgin birth of Christ, the physical resurrection, the inerrancy of Scripture, the substitutionary atonement, and the imminent, physical second coming of Christ. Millions of copies were distributed free, and those who subscribed to the doctrines set forth in them came to be known as "fundamentalists." With increasing intensity a controversy raged between fundamentalists and liberals, or modernists, in almost all religious bodies of the land, but it was especially divisive in Baptist and Presbyterian circles. Several splits resulted in those denominations, launching such denominations or movements as the Orthodox Presbyterians, the Bible Presbyterians, the General Association of Regular Baptists, the Conservative Baptist Association, the North American Baptist Association, and the Independent Fundamental Churches of America. And a host of churches all over the land went independent as community churches, Bible churches, or independent Baptist churches.

For a long time fundamentalists were known as negative or combative and anti-intellectual, but a great many of them have developed more positive attitudes in recent years and have built hundreds of Bible colleges, liberal arts colleges, and theological seminaries all over the world. Early in the century they tended to neglect social ministries, somewhat in reaction to the Social Gospel. But that observation has been considerably overdrawn, because they have always supported rescue missions, children's homes, and many other home missions projects, in addition to an incalculable number of hospitals, clinics, schools, and other philanthropic works all over the world. Educational systems in many areas of developing countries owe their existence to these conservative Christian groups.

Second, there has come a basic change in outlook in the Christianity of recent decades. During the latter part of the nineteenth century and the early part of the twentieth, optimism pervaded Christianity. In liberal circles this was expressed in terms of the perfectability of human nature and the idea that man was improving. Ultimately a utopian state would be reached. The Darwinian concept of evolution and the striking number of new inventions that promised a better future for mankind gave credence to that view. In more conservative circles this optimism was expressed in terms of postmillennialism, according to which it was thought that the gospel would pervade all of society and bring in a reign of righteousness on earth. Two world wars, a devastating depression, German inhumanity toward the Jews, widespread purges of dissenters by the Communists in lands they took over, and a world divided between two powers engaged in a nuclear arms race have virtually annihilated the old utopian or millennial dreams and the concept of perfectability of human nature. Increasingly, man is viewed as being incurably bad. Pessimism has become the creed of the day in many circles. Oswald Spengler's *Decline of the West*, written in 1918, expresses this pessimism.

With the change from optimism to pessimism or realism has come a change in attitude toward the Bible. As a result of archaeological and historical study, it has become increasingly clear to scholars and laymen that the Bible is an essentially accurate historical document. The views of such higher critical schools as Wellhausen and Tübingen moderated greatly. In fact, liberalism in general has become more moderate in attitude toward the Scripture.

As the old optimism died and as the old liberalism moderated, it also became clear that the antisupernaturalism of previous generations was inadequate for a day when the very foundations of society seemed to be quivering. Some churchmen said, "We have removed the supernatural from the Bible; we have humanized the person of Christ; we have emptied the churches—now what?" The answer for many seemed to be neo-orthodoxy. Led by Karl Barth and Emil Brunner, neo-orthodoxy provided a via media between the old conservatism and the old liberalism. While holding on to some of the higher critical views of Scripture on the one hand, it stressed on the other hand a supernaturalism, the virgin birth, and a sinful humanity who needed salvation; and many of them spoke of the substitutionary death of Christ. God was viewed as the transcendent one, the wholly other, who breaks in on human beings in a crisis experience. The Bible, while fallible, *contained* the word of God and *became* the word of God whenever it spoke to the reader. In other words, neo-orthodoxy confused revelation with illumination, which is the Spirit's ministry in teaching through the Word. Because neo-orthodox theologians tended to use the same vocabulary as conservatives but poured new meaning into common terms, often it was not clear exactly what they did believe.

Karl Barth (1886-1968) was the leading spokesman of the movement. Born in Basel, he studied in Switzerland and Germany and became a pastor in Switzerland. He found that his liberal theology offered little hope for people gripped in the horrors of war, and in 1919 he broke with liberalism in the publication of his commentary on Romans. Thereafter, he taught in German universities until expelled by the Nazis in 1930. Then he returned to Basel to teach. Though he wrote over five hundred books and articles, his commentary on Romans and his four-volume *Church Dogmatics*, produced late in life, are among his most important works. His views changed over the years, but his teaching of a sovereign God who spoke to people through the written word did not. Barth viewed man as sinful and spoke of Christ's dying and suffering rejection for all so all might be redeemed in Him. At times this teaching seemed to border on universalism, but Barth denied that he taught universalism. Eventually Barth found that he satisfied neither conservatives nor liberals, but his influence was, nevertheless, very great indeed. He seems to have been closer to the conservative position on the virgin birth, the resurrection of Christ, and other cardinal doctrines than were Brunner and the Niebuhrs.

Emil Brunner (1889-1966) was also a Swiss theologian; he eventually broke with Barth because he put more stock in natural theology than Barth did. Independently of Barth he reevaluated his liberal views during World War I. Ultimately he came to view revelation as personal encounter with God, who communicates Himself. Many of his views were similar to those of Barth; but he differed with Barth in holding that God may be known partially through nature, and he held that the image of God in man is not completely lost.

The leading American exponent of neo-orthodoxy was Reinhold Niebuhr (1893-1971). While a pastor in Detroit, he developed an interest in social and economic problems and carried this interest with him in his long professorship at Union Theological Seminary in New York. He wrote seventeen major books, among which were *Moral Man and Immoral Society* and *Faith and History*. Like Barth, he saw God as the "wholly other" and believed that society needed drastic changes; but he differed with Barth's lack of social concern. He believed that God's encounter with man would enable man to overcome his sin of pride and selfishness and to achieve good in a sinful society. Niebuhr helped to found Americans for Democratic Action and the National Council of Churches.

Another major representative of American neo-orthodoxy was H. Richard Niebuhr (1894-1962), Reinhold's younger brother and the more scholarly of the two. Among his several books produced during his professorship at Yale was *The Kingdom of God in America*, in which he moved away from his earlier liberalism and looked for a restoration of Reformation roots in American society.

Neo-orthodoxy nearly conquered Protestant Europe in the 1930s and 1940s and made a determined bid for control of American theological schools. Gradually, Bultmann and Tillich took over some of the territory Barth had controlled.

Rudolf Bultmann made a tremendous impact on the theological scene in the late 1940s and 1950s. He spoke of the need to "demythologize" the concepts of the New Testament and showed himself skeptical of the historical content of the gospels. Yet he did not abandon a need for some kind of decision for Jesus Christ, even though he was not at all clear on what one should base the decision.

Paul Tillich's theological influence was especially great in the 1950s and 1960s. His beliefs are difficult to put into simple language, because his views were based on Platonism, mysticism, and existentialism. He understood God as the "Ground of Being"; man derives his own being by participation existentially in the "Ground of Being." Many accused him of holding to a kind of pantheism and an impersonal deity. He also taught that it was only through the myths or symbols of Scripture that man could grasp or understand God, the "Ground of Being." Barth, Bultmann, and Tillich were all in one way or another products of existentialism: they tended to split religious experience from objective, scientific knowledge.

During the 1960s, as a kind of fallout of Tillich and a reaction to Barth, the "God is dead" movement developed. In a sense its adherents were saying, "We have lost special revelation entirely if we don't have the Barthian experience with God." That is to say, if the Bible only becomes the Word of God when He speaks through it, if there is a word of God only when God speaks in the existential moment or in the crisis experience, then when God does not speak there is no word of God. Therefore, it is impossible to know God. So they became intellectual agnostics and a few of them atheists. The most important men in the American movement were Thomas J. J. Altizer, William Hamilton, Paul Van Buren, and Harvey Cox.

In the later 1960s and 1970s, the influence of neo-orthodoxy waned, and there was a shift to both the right and the left. On the right, there was a new worldwide acceptance of a literal approach to Scripture. Certainly this is the position of evangelicalism in general in the United States, of the worldwide Pentecostal movement, of the great revival and missionary movements of Latin America and Africa and the Far East, of the great following of Billy Graham, and of many others in the world. Though neo-orthodoxy is no longer the dominant force it was at seminaries and universities, it influences many who follow a kind of middle way in their view of Christianity and the Scripture. On the left is process theology. This is a kind of neoliberalism with an emphasis on the immanence of God. There is no absolute authority. The Bible has value along with other religious texts. This system is a kind of synthesis of everything theological that has been going on during the 1950s and 1960s. God Himself as well as the universe is in the process of "becoming." Absoluteness of being is denied. Becoming is the ultimate category.

So, many in Christendom are traveling the paths of a threadbare liberalism today. They will find no more vitality in their pursuits than their forebears who trod the same lanes when they had different names. Disillusioned, some of them will leave the church, others will continue to go through the motions of playing at church, and yet others will return to the authority of the Bible and its life-giving message.

A current theological movement that has arisen primarily in Latin America but has numerous North American exponents is liberation theology.[6] It originated in 1965, the year that Vatican II finished its work. At that time fifteen Roman Catholic bishops, speaking on behalf of Third World nations, affirmed that the church should unite with all the exploited in those peoples' efforts to recover their rights; that property should have a collective destiny; and that the church should not be "attached to financial imperialisms." Liberation theology endeavored to erect a system of theology based on such presuppositions. The Peruvian theologian Gustavo Gutierrez wrote the most systematic account of the movement in his *A Theology of Liberation* (1973). As the movement has developed, it has attracted Roman Catholics and Protestants with widely varying viewpoints on how the needs of humanity are to be met and how Scripture is to be used. Therefore it is almost impossible to generalize with any degree of

6. Especially useful books on liberation theology include Robert McAfee Brown, *Theology in a New Key* (Philadelphia: Westminster, 1978); Orlando E. Costas, *Christ Outside the Gate* (Maryknoll, New York: Orbis, 1982); Rosino Gibellini, ed., *Frontiers of Theology in Latin America* (Maryknoll; New York: Orbis, 1975); J. Andrew Kirk, *Liberation Theology* (Atlanta: John Knox, 1979) and *Theology Encounters Revolution* (Downers Grove, Ill.: Inter-Varsity, 1980); and Gerald H. Anderson and Thomas F. Stransky, eds., *Mission Trends No. 4: Liberation Theologies in North America and Europe* (Grand Rapids: Eerdmans, 1979).

accuracy as to what the *theologies* of liberation teach. What follows should be taken as a broad approximation of some facets of the movement; in each case there are nearly as many nuances of opinion as there are spokesmen involved.

Generally speaking, liberation theologians start with historical reality rather than with propositional truth as revealed in the Bible; and they have a tendency to find in the social sciences the tools for a construction of theology. For them the most important reality of life, especially as it is viewed in Latin America, is that humanity is oppressed and in need of liberation. The oppression is analyzed in Marxist terms, as resulting from the vested interests of capitalist power structures. At least most of the leading spokesmen believe existing structures must be destroyed in order to free humanity.

Liberation theology's view of human nature normally is rather optimistic; human beings are thought of as capable of improving society and are not considered to be as sinful as the Bible says they are. The attention to salvation from political, social, and economic oppression causes these thinkers to ignore the need for spiritual salvation and release from bondage to sin. Frequently salvation is viewed as a collective matter, concerning the whole of society instead of the individual. Liberation theologians place heavy emphasis on the Bible's teaching concerning the poor, which they commonly conclude refers to the sociologically poor. And they tend to ignore the religiously or spiritually poor, which includes all mankind. The positive uses of suffering and suffering as judgment are largely overlooked in the rush to eliminate all suffering.

The supernatural gets short shrift in liberation theology. The ministry of the Holy Spirit, prayer, and pietistic concerns generally are incidental. In the hands of most liberation theologians the Bible no longer is a fixed absolute from which flow the truths concerning salvation and Christian conduct. The place of the church in the life of the believer is ignored or marginalized. Jesus as teacher and messiah (small *m*) often is presented as a violent reactor to all forms of social and political oppression, and appears more in the role of a Judas Maccabeus than the ruler of a new spiritual kingdom.

Liberation theology has an anti-American bias and almost seems to conclude that the United States cannot do anything right, even though Americans help feed two-thirds of the world and are still considered by many of the world's oppressed and poor as the greatest hope for relief. Most of the world's oppressed would favorably entertain the thought of moving to the United States if that were possible.

Liberation theology tends to be blind to bondage and oppression anywhere except in Central and South America; it needs to be more ecumenical in its humanistic sympathy. It commonly ignores victims of Soviet and Eastern European oppression, Cuban exiles, and black victims of black dictators in Africa because by definition socialist countries cannot oppress. Moreover, the selective thinking of liberation theologians leads many of them to adopt an idealized vision of Marxism that ignores the weaknesses or failures of Marxist economic systems.

Liberation theologians generally see poverty as produced by exploitation, which comes from local and international capitalism. Multinational corporations often bear the brunt of the attack. The solution to the problem commonly is thought to be overthrow of the economic system. Normally there is no patience with technocrats who argue that the real problem is lack of education or managerial skill, the lack of productivity, or the lack of capital. Without a knowledge of history, liberation theologians blame capitalism for a situation created by Spanish and Portuguese feudal economic and social systems erected at the time of colonization—long before the impact of capitalism.

Evangelicals worry that liberation theology tends to desupernaturalize the Bible, to politicize Christ, to ignore the need for personal and spiritual salvation, to present a slightly spiritualized Marxism, and merely to recast the old social gospel in a new form. They observe that if all the social and economic ills of Latin America were solved without proper attention to spiritual needs, the region would be no better off spiritually than it is now; life involves more than social and political freedom and two cars in every garage. Moreover, patriotic Americans find its anti-American bias distasteful.

But liberation theology does take a more holistic view of humanity, considering physical and psychological needs along with the spiritual, than evangelicals often have done. And it reminds the church that if it expects to be heard in the present and the future it will have to come to grips with human suffering even more than it has in recent years. Almost half the world's population lives in countries where the per capita income is less than 250 American dollars per year. Two-thirds of the people of the world are desperately undernourished; according to Food for the Hungry, 40,000 per day, or almost 15 million per year, die of starvation and malnutrition. Twenty-two of the 36 poorest nations in the world are located in sub-Saharan Africa, and Africa is the only region where per capita food production has declined during the last two years. Over 800 million people of the world are considered to be destitute. Armed conflict, drought, severe depression, and political oppression have forced millions from their homes. All this adds up to a world awash with refugees debilitated by malnutrition, weakened and destroyed by illness, deprived of adequate housing, and prevented from getting adequate education.

The world is in dire physical need; its spiritual need is even greater. By the most generous total of all branches of Christendom, there are well over 3 billion unreached with the gospel of Jesus Christ. Moreover, as the population increase has accelerated more rapidly in the traditionally non-Christian parts of the world than in the more heavily Christian sectors, and as public policy in many lands has restricted Christian outreach, the percentage of Christians in the world apparently has been declining slightly but steadily since 1900.

Many in the American evangelical camp must realize that they have become too insulated by a comfortable orthodoxy. The growing respectability of evangelical Christianity and the effects of materialism have lulled a host of them into a lethargic state. A large percentage of evangelicals have too little spiritual power and too little impact for good on the society around them. In the midst of moral and social decay, they provide too little salt with its preservative quality or too little of the light of the gospel. And in a land surfeited with biblical literature of all kinds, ignorance of the Word of God is abysmal. There seems to be far too little evidence of the power of the gospel to affect life-style. Alcoholism, an increasing divorce rate, and other social evils plague the church as they do society in general. There is little individual concern for living a holy life. Thus the church utters a muffled or uncertain sound instead of a clear and prophetic voice to a confused and dying world. It is time for an agonizing reappraisal. It is time for the church of Jesus Christ to be up and doing.

Books for Further Study

A select list of works widely available in libraries and book stores is thought to be more valuable to the reader than an extensive bibliography or a number of primary source works. Because many readers have special interest in the American scene (including revivalism) or the Reformation, the bibliography has separate sections for each of these areas, as well as a general section.

General

Bainton, Roland H. *The Medieval Church.* New York: Van Nostrand, 1926.

Barrett, David. *World Christian Encyclopedia.* Oxford: Oxford U., 1982.

Bettenson, Henry, ed. *Documents of the Christian Church.* 2d ed. New York: 1963.

Cairns, Earle E. *Christianity Through the Centuries.* Rev. ed. Grand Rapids: Zondervan, 1981.

Cross, F. L., ed. *Oxford Dictionary of the Christian Church.* Rev. ed. New York: Oxford, 1974.

Detzler, Wayne A. *The Changing Church in Europe.* Grand Rapids: Zondervan, 1979.

Douglas, J. D., ed. *The New International Dictionary of the Christian Church.* Grand Rapids: Zondervan, 1974.

Eerdman's Handbook to the History of Christianity. Grand Rapids: Eerdmans, 1977.

Falk, Peter. *The Growth of the Church in Africa.* Grand Rapids: Zondervan, 1978.

Gail, Marzieh. *Avignon in Flower.* London: Victor Gollancz, 1966.

Grousset, René. *The Epic of the Crusades.* New York: Orion, 1970.

Heick, Otto W. *A History of Christian Thought.* 2 vols. Philadelphia: Fortress, 1965.

Hill, Bennett D., ed. *Church and State in the Middle Ages.* New York: Wiley, 1970.

Hoke, Donald E., ed. *The Church in Asia.* Chicago: Moody, 1975.

Latourette, Kenneth S. *A History of Christianity.* Rev. ed. 2 vols. New York: Harper & Row, 1975.

Meyer, Carl S. *The Church from Pentecost to the Present.* Chicago: Moody, 1969.

O'Brien, John M. *The Medieval Church.* Totowa, N.J.: Littlefield, Adams, 1968.

Pernoud, Régine. *The Crusades.* London: Oliver & Boyd, 1963.

Renwick, A. M. *The Story of the Church.* Grand Rapids: Eerdmans, 1958.

Schaff, Philip. *History of the Christian Church.* 8 vols. New York: Scribner's, 1910. Reprint. Grand Rapids: Eerdmans, 1960.

Southern, R. W. *Western Society and the Church in the Middle Ages.* Grand Rapids: Eerdmans, 1970.

Tucker, Ruth. *From Jerusalem to Irian Jaya.* Grand Rapids: Zondervan, 1983.

Walker, Williston. *A History of the Christian Church.* 3d ed. New York: Scribner's, 1970.

The Reformation

Bainton, Roland, *Here I Stand.* New York: New American Library, 1950.

———. *The Reformation of the Sixteenth Century.* Boston: Beacon Hill, 19⌄2.

———. *Women of the Reformation*. Minneapolis: Augsburg, 1971.

Daniel-Rops, H. *The Catholic Reformation*. New York: Dutton, 1962.

Dickens, A. G. *The English Reformation*. New York: Schocken, 1964.

Farner, Oskar. *Zwingli the Reformer*. New York: Philosophical Library, 1952.

Grimm, Harold J. *The Reformation Era*. Rev. ed. New York: Macmillan, 1965.

Holl, Karl. *The Cultural Significance of the Reformation*. Cleveland: World, 1959.

McNeill, John T. *The History and Character of Calvinism*. New York: Oxford, 1954.

Mosse, George L. *The Reformation*. 3d ed. New York: Holt, Rinehart, 1963.

Ozment, Steven E. *The Reformation in the Cities*. New Haven, Conn.: Yale U., 1975.

Powicke, Maurice. *The Reformation in England*. London: Oxford, 1941.

Rabb, Theodore, *The Thirty Years War*. 2d ed. Lexington, Mass.: Heath, 1972.

Reid, W. Stanford, ed. *The Reformation—Revival or Revolution?* New York: Holt, Rinehart, 1968.

Ridley, Jasper, *John Knox*. New York: Oxford, 1968.

Rilliet, Jean. *Zwingli, Third Man of the Reformation*. Philadelphia: Westminster, 1964.

Ritter, Gerhard. *Luther*. New York: Harper & Row, 1963.

Schwiebert, Ernest. *Luther and His Times*. St. Louis: Concordia, 1950.

Spinka, Matthew. *John Hus*. Princeton: Princeton U., 1968.

Wedgewood, C. V. *The Thirty Years War*. Harmondsworth, England: Penguin, 1957.

Williams, George H. *The Radical Reformation*. Philadelphia: Westminster, 1962.

The American Church

Ahlstrom, Sydney. *A Religious History of the American People*. Garden City, N.Y.: Doubleday, 1975.

Banks, William. *The Black Church in the United States*. Chicago: Moody, 1972.

Bedell, George, et. al. *Religion in America*. New York: Macmillan, 1975.

Brauer, Jerald. *Protestantism in America*. Philadelphia: Westminster, 1972.

Bushman, Richard. *The Great Awakening*. New York: Norton, 1972.

Cairns, Earle E. *Christianity in the United States*. Chicago: Moody, 1964.

Gaustad, Edwin S. *The Great Awakening in New England*. Gloucester, Mass.: Peter Smith, 1965.

──────. *A Religious History of America*. New York: Harper & Row, 1966.

Gewehr, Wesley. *The Great Awakening in Virginia*. Gloucester, Mass.: Peter Smith, 1930.

Heimert, Alan. *Religion and the American Mind*. Cambridge, Mass.: Harvard, 1966.

Jacquet, Constant H., ed. *Yearbook of American and Canadian Churches*. Nashville: Abingdon, published annually.

Maxson, Charles. *The Great Awakening in the Middle Colonies*. Gloucester, Mass.: Peter Smith, 1920.

Mead, Frank S. *Handbook of Denominations in the United States*. 6th ed. New York: Abingdon, 1975.

Olmstead, Clifton E. *History of Religion in the United States*. Rev. ed. Englewood Cliffs, N.J.: Prentice-Hall, 1960.

Orr, J. Edwin. *Campus Aflame*. Glendale, Cal.: Regal, 1972.

──────. *Eager Feet*. Chicago: Moody, 1975.

──────. *Fervent Prayer*. Chicago: Moody, 1974.

──────. *Flaming Tongue*. 2d ed. Chicago: Moody, 1975.

Smith, Timothy L. *Revivalism and Social Reform: American Protestantism on the Eve of the Civil War*. Magnolia, Mass.: Peter Smith, n.d.

Sweet, William W. *Religion in Colonial America*. New York: Cooper Square, 1942.

──────. *The Story of Religion in America*. Twin Brooks Series. Rev. ed. New York: Harper, 1950. Reprint. Grand Rapids: Baker, 1973.

General Index

Alexandria, school of, 15
Ambrose of Milan, 18, 54
American Bible Society, 139, 175-76
Anabaptists, 92-94
Anglican Church, 100-102, 121-22, 128-30, 133-34, 137, 162-63
Antoninus Pius, 12, 26
Apologists, 10-13
Apostles' Creed, 41
Apostles, tradition concerning ministry of, 4-5
Apostolic Fathers, 7-10
Aquinas, 69
Arius, 42, 45
Arminianism, 116-17, 121
Arminius, Jacobus, 116-17
Asbury, Francis, 136
Assemblies of God, 165, 186-87

Athanasius, 17, 39, 42-43
Augustine, of England, 55
Augustine, of Hippo, 19, 45-46, 54, 77
Augustinians, 70, 84
Avignon, 73, 77

Babylonian Captivity of papacy, 72
Backus, Isaac, 138
Bacon, Francis, 118
Baptists, 102, 134, 136, 138-39, 141, 143, 165-68
Barnabas, 3, 9
Barth, Karl, 194-95
Basil of Caesarea, 20, 55
Bede, 58
Benedict IX (pope), 61
Bernard of Clairvaux, 65, 69-70
Bible college movement, 168

in Netherlands, 105-7
in Scandinavia, 89-90
in Scotland, 103-5
in Switzerland, 90-97
Renaissance, 71-73, 81-82
Richelieu, 110
Ritschl, Albert, 145-46
Roman Catholics (in
    Maryland), 129
Romanticism, 122
Rutgers College, 136

Saint Bartholomew's
    Massacre, 99
St. Benedict, 55, 70
St. Francis, Franciscans, 70
St. Patrick, 55
Salvation Army, 126
Sankey, Ira D., 141
Savonarola, Girolamo, 79
Saul of Tarsus, 3. *See also*
    Paul
Schleiermacher, Friedrich,
    122, 146
Scholasticism, 68-69, 117
Seabury, Samuel, 134
Second Evangelical
    Awakening, 138-39
Separation of church and
    state (U.S.), 131-33
Servetus, Michael, 95-96
Seventh-Day Adventists, 148
Shepherd of Hermas, 8
Simony, 64
Slavery, and the churches, 140-
    43, 145
Smith, Henry P., 147
Socinus, Faustus;
    Socinianism, 117

Southern Baptists, 143, 165-67
Spener, P. J., 116
Spiritualism, 148
Stephen, 2-3
Stephen (king), 61
Swedenborg, Emanuel, 114-15
Symmachus, 52
Synod of Dort, 116
Synod of Whitby, 56

Tappan, Arthur, 142
Tatian, 13, 40
Taylor, J. Hudson, 123
Television ministry, 172-73
Temperance movement, 144
Tennent, Gilbert, 135
Tennent, William, 135
Tertullian, 13-14, 32
Theodore, 20
Thirty Years War, 109-11, 113
Three Great Cappodocians, 20
Tillich, Paul, 196
Trajan, 26
Transubstantiation, 67
Treaty of Verdun, 60
Tyrrell, George, 147

Unitarians, 33, 137, 139, 145-
    46
United Church of Canada, 161,
    165
United Church of Christ, 161-
    62, 165, 170
Unity of the Brethren. *See*
    Moravians
Urban II, 65

Valerian, 28
Vatican Council I, 125